Journal of Child and Youth Care

1991 Special Issue

Child Sexual Abuse

ISBN 0-919813-97-6
ISSN 0840-982X
University of Calgary Press
2500 University Drive N.W.
Calgary, Alberta, Canada T2N 1N4

Canadian Cataloguing in Publication Data

Main entry under title:
Child sexual abuse

Special issue of the Journal of child and youth care.
ISBN 0-919813-97-6

1. Sexually abused children. 2. Sexually abused children--Services for. I. Thomlison, B. (Barbara). II. Bagley, Christopher. III. Title: Journal of child and youth care.
HQ71.C54 1991 362.7'6 C91-091669-1

Cover design and layout by Rhae Ann Bromley
Text design by Visual Communications Consulting
Typography by Eileen Eckert
Printed and bound in Canada by Hignell Printing, Ltd.

∞ This book is printed on acid-free paper.

CONTENTS

In This Issue

This issue contains selected papers presented at a University of Calgary workshop on research and therapy in the field of child sexual abuse, which explains why so many of the contributors are from the academic and professional community in Calgary. In recent years, Calgary has become a leading centre in the humane and integrated treatment of victims of child sexual abuse, and their families. A well-coordinated and well-funded child protection system in Calgary and the surrounding rural area works in collaboration with police, crown prosecutors, and therapists. Long-term therapy for victims, their families, and offenders is contracted out to a variety of agencies. One of these practices, the humanistic mode of therapy, was described by Anderson and Mayes (1982) in a previous issue of this journal. Another model, described in the present issue by Robbie Babins-Wagner, practices a modified form of family systems therapy. There are a half dozen different agencies in Calgary operating on different theoretical assumptions, and accepting different kinds of referral. In this pluralistic model, it is assumed that the best fit can usually be made between client need and therapeutic system.

One of the problems in organizing a system of therapy for both victims and their abusers is the unpredictability of judges: there is no guarantee that a man who pleads guilty to sexual assault upon his child will receive a short sentence in a provincial prison, or a suspended sentence, which would allow therapy to be ongoing. We know from the work of Stephens and his colleagues (published in this issue) that a man is most likely to be brought to trial, and to be found guilty, if he admits the offence. And only a minority of cases in which social workers are certain that sexual abuse has taken place, result in the prosecution of the assumed offender. Non-prosecution is most likely when the offender denies the action.

An interesting model of practice has emerged from Hinton in Northern Alberta (Bagley, 1988). Here a single judge has evolved a system which encourages maximum cooperation by offenders. The offender will be charged, but will not be brought to trial until *after* a period of mandated therapy for the victim. If the man cooperates in this therapy, and apologizes to his victim, he will receive only a two-year suspended sentence. External evaluation of this program indicates that a suspended sentence is more effective in deterring any further offence than probation. The reason why this excellent cooperation between judges and treatment agencies cannot be deployed in larger cities such as Edmonton or Calgary is because there are diverse and conflicting opinions amongst judges themselves about what kind of charging and sentencing might be appropriate. It is likely that some offenders might risk a lengthy prison term by denying the offence (and causing further harm to their victim) when they know that admission is likely to result, in say, a three-year custodial term. Other things being equal, the more punitive society is towards offenders, the more likely it is that offenders will deny their actions. There is clearly a need for both federal and provincial action in this area to initiate reform. The federal government has made a number of important legal changes in response to the Badgley and Rogers' recommendations (see the review article in this issue); but more needs to be done in this legal domain.

Finally, it is obvious that prevention is better than cure. Helping young children to recognize the signs of abuse, to avoid it, and to report it as soon as it begins, is an excellent strategy, and Lesley Tutty's article in this issue provides important information and analysis in this regard. And, it is possible also to recognize and treat young males in residential child and youth care, who have experienced prior sexual abuse, and are in danger of moving into the victim-to-abuser cycle, as Bagley and Shewchuk-Dann, Baird, and Orr stress in this issue.

REFERENCES

Anderson, C., & Mayes, P. (1982). Treating family sexual abuse: The humanistic approach. *Journal of Child and Youth Care, 1*(2), 31–46.

Bagley, C. (1988). Integrated treatment of child sexual abuse. *The Advocate: Journal of the Alberta Association of Social Workers, 13*(4), 1–4.

This publication has been funded by support from the Calgary Society for the Prevention of Child Sexual Abuse, and the Faculty of Social Work at the University of Calgary.

Journal of Child and Youth Care Special Issue Pages 1 – 6
 ISSN 0840–982X

Male Victims of Child Sexual Abuse: A Brief Overview of Pertinent Findings

Mark Genuis, Barbara Thomlison, and Christopher Bagley
Faculty of Social Work, The University of Calgary

The extent of the sexual misuse and exploitation of children has only been recognized by policy makers and human service professionals since the mid-1970s (Bagley & Thurston, 1988). Prior to this time, sexual abuse was assumed either to occur rarely and be of no consequence to the child victim, to have existed only in the child's fantasy, or to have been provoked by the child (Bagley & King, 1990). We now know that such generalizations were grossly unfair, and were part of the syndrome of "blaming the victim."

Since the mid-1970s numerous studies have reported significant and lasting detrimental psychological effects of sexual abuse on the victims (Bagley & Thomlison, 1991; Baker & Duncan, 1985; Courtois, 1979; Genuis & Violato, 1991). Many children with emotional and behavioural problems have experienced prior abuse, which has a direct link with their present disorders (Steele, 1986). The extent and effects of sexual abuse of female children is now becoming well understood. Accordingly, rapid improvements have been made in both prevention and education programs to the point where at least one recent study has reported the overall prevalence of child sexual abuse of females in Canada may be declining (Bagley, 1990).

Most of the research and program development in this field has addressed the abuse of females, leaving our knowledge of the prevalence of abuse and the extent of the psychological effects on male victims fairly rudimentary (Briere, 1989). The study of male child sexual abuse is still in an exploratory stage (Violato & Genuis, 1991), but the reported findings present certain consistent trends which allow us to conclude that at least four percent of male children are victims of sexual abuse

(Finkelhor, 1985), and that such abuse has existed for at least as long as the present century (Bagley, 1988; Bagley & Thomlison, 1991).

In a review of published research, Violato and Genuis (1991) reported numerous initial and long-term psychological effects to male victims of child sexual abuse. They also reported that the majority of perpetrators are adult males, but that the actual percentages of male versus female perpetrators are not clear, and nor are the specific perpetrator/victim relationships well understood.

The victim/perpetrator cycle for male victims of child sexual abuse is consistently discussed in the literature (Violato & Genuis, 1991). Two recent studies gathered data specifically related to the victim/perpetrator cycle and both reported that prior victims were significantly more likely to, or were already sexually abusing children, than were males who were not victims of sexual abuse (Briere & Runtz, 1989; Genuis & Violato, 1991). The article in this issue by Bagley and Shewchuk-Dann demonstrates the clinical parameters of the victim/perpetrator cycle and the possibilities for the intervention of professionals working with children.

Lew (1990) argued that men can help one another in the recovery process, and that the descent in the victim/perpetrator cycle is by no means inevitable. Lew's volume is an excellent handbook for those counselling groups for former victims.

A GLANCE AT THE LITERATURE ON MALE VICTIMS

The study of the sexual abuse of male children is in a state of disarray (Violato & Genuis, 1991). This is in part due to a paucity of both empirical and clinical evidence. Moreover, since this nascent area has seen primarily exploratory studies, there are no standard definitions or methodologies. Disparate definitions have been used to operationalize abuse and a variety of designs to collect data have been employed (Bagley & Thurston, 1988; Violato & Genuis, 1991). As a result, findings from the different studies are either not comparable or contradict each other. Although patterns of abuse of effects from the abuse are present within the literature, it is not yet appropriate to draw conclusions from the available studies.

Aspects of sexual abuse discussed here include (1) definitions, (2) prevalence, victim profiles, and abuse type, (3) home background, and (4) outcomes.

Definitions

One of the main problems in the area of sexual abuse is the variations of the definitions of child sexual abuse used by different researchers (Greenburg, 1979; Browne & Finkelhor, 1986; Violato & Genuis, 1991). Some studies have defined sexual abuse as including both contact and no-contact acts (Baker & Duncan, 1985) and others have required a certain age difference between the perpetrator and victim in order to define an act as sexual abuse (Fromuth & Burkhart, 1989). Fromuth and Burkhart (1989) argued that the age difference was necessary in order to avoid including cases of sexual experimentation between children. Adolescents do sexually abuse children at various ages, however (Davis & Leitenberg, 1987). Therefore, the requirement that the perpetrator be five years older than the victim appears inadequate for inclusion within a definition of child sexual abuse. The involvement of both contact and non-contact acts is very broad and includes a large variety of acts. Such a definition is unclear as it does not clearly define sexual abuse for the subjects, and is therefore difficult for researchers to measure and compare cases.

The clearest and yet not overly restrictive definition is provided by unwanted contact. The criterion stressing unwanted sexual contact appears to be a better method of eliminating cases of consensual sex play among peers than some arbitrary age criterion. Therefore, we recommend that for research purposes, child sexual abuse be operationalized as unwanted sexual contact (genital and fondling through to intercourse) while the victim is considered a child by legal definition. Using this definition, varying community standards are considered (Bagley, 1991; Violato & Genuis, 1991).

Prevalence, Victim Profile, and Abuse Types

Reports on prevalence range from four percent (Finkelhor, 1985) to 16 percent (Fromuth & Burkhart, 1989). In their review, Violato and Genuis (1991) estimated the prevalence rate of male sexual abuse to be 10 percent. The estimate by Violato and Genuis (1991) may be an underestimate because of underreporting. As well as underreporting, varying estimates reflect differences in definition, age selection, questions used, method, and population surveyed. There is also disagreement between studies about the average age of male victims at the time of onset of sexual abuse, as well as the duration, extent, and nature of the abuse, as well as others (Finkelhor, 1982, 1985; Fritz, Stoll & Wagner, 1981; Meiselman, 1986; Pierce & Pierce, 1985; Reinhart, 1987; Risin & Koss, 1987; Spencer & Dunklee, 1986; Vander-Mey, 1988).

Home Background

Male victims of child sexual abuse are more likely than males in the general population to come from homes marked by alcoholism and personality disorder in either or both parents, disruption of family relationships, excessive physical punishment and emotional neglect (Burgess, Hartman & McCormack, 1987; Cooper & Cormier, 1982; Davis & Leitenberg, 1987; Finkelhor, 1982; Meiselman, 1986; Vander-Mey, 1988).

Outcomes

The following is a summary of factors, many of which are the same as those experienced initially, associated with child sexual abuse in the long-term: low self-esteem, depression, learned helplessness, attribution of locus of control to external factors, confusion regarding sexual orientation, guilt, alienation, distrust, homosexual tendencies, victim/perpetrator cycle, problems in psychosexual relations, becoming a neglectful and/or abusive caretaker, multiple personalities, sexual masochism, asthma, frigidity, promiscuity, eating disorders, self-harm, addictions, prostitution, obesity, epilepsy, and increased acceptance of pain (Violato & Genuis, 1991). Many researchers have speculated causal links between the abuse and these factors. It is not likely, however, that sexual abuse alone could lead to this array of psychopathology. A more likely explanation may be that many victims of child sexual abuse are raised in environments which are very traumatic where other deleterious conditions interact with the sexual abuse to result in the aforementioned pathologies.

SUMMARY

The foregoing discussion affirms that sexual abuse of male children is an issue which requires much more research in order to gain understanding about the predictors and outcomes of the abuse, as well as to establish effective treatment programs. The articles in this special edition address these issues in varying degrees. It is hoped that this initial examination of various aspects of male victims of child sexual abuse can assist practitioner and researcher alike, and indicate some important trends that are beginning to emerge from the data. In particular, the reader is directed to Thomlison, Stephens, Cunes, Grinell and Krysik, Baird, and Orr in this issue for further data on male victims of child sexual abuse.

REFERENCES

Bagley, C. (1988). *Child sexual abuse in national Canadian survey.* Ottawa: Department of Health and Welfare.

Bagley, C. (1990). Is the prevalence of child sexual abuse decreasing? Evidence from a random sample of 750 young adult women. *Psychological Reports, 66,* 1037–1038.

Bagley, C. (in press). The prevalence and mental health sequels of child sexual abuse in a community sample of women aged 18 to 27. *Canadian Journal of Community of Mental Health.*

Bagley, C., & King, K. (1990). *Child sexual abuse: The search for healing.* London: Routledge.

Bagley, C., & Thomlison, R. (1991). *Child sexual abuse: Critical perspectives on prevention, intervention and treatment.* Toronto: Wall & Emerson.

Bagley, C., & Thurston, W. (1988). *Child sexual abuse: Critical reviews of the research literature.* Ottawa: Federal Health and Welfare.

Baker, A.W., & Duncan, S.P. (1985). Child sexual abuse: A study of prevalence in Great Britain. *Child Abuse and Neglect, 9,* 457–467.

Briere, J. (1989). *Therapy with adult survivors of child sexual abuse.* New York: Guilford Press.

Briere, J., & Runtz, M. (1989). University males' sexual interest in children: Predicting potential indices of "pedophilia" in a nonforensic sample. *Child Abuse and Neglect, 13,* 65–75.

Browne, A., & Finkelhor, D. (1986). Impact of child sexual abuse: A review of the research. *Psychological Bulletin, 99*(1), 66–77.

Burgess, A., Hartman, C., & McCormack, A. (1987). Abused to abuser: Antecedents of socially deviant behaviors. *American Journal of Psychiatry, 144,* 1431–1436.

Cooper, L., & Cormier, B. (1982). Inter-generational transmission of incest. *Canadian Journal of Psychiatry, 27,* 231–235.

Courtois, C.A. (1979). Characteristics of a volunteer sample of adult women who experienced incest in childhood or adolescence. *Dissertation Abstracts International, 40*(6-A), 3194–3195.

Davis, C., & Leitenberg, H. (1987). Adolescent sex offenders. *Psychological Bulletin, 101,* 417–427.

Finkelhor, D. (1984). Boys as victims: Review of the evidence (chapter 10, pp. 150–170). In D. Finkelhor, (Ed.), *Child sexual abuse: New theory and research.*. New York: Free Press.

Finkelhor, D. (1985). Sexual abuse of boys. In A. Burgess (Ed.), *Rape and sexual assault: A research handbook* (pp. 97–109). New York: Garland.

Fritz, G., Stoll, K., & Wagner, N. (1981). A comparison of males and females who were sexually molested as children. *Journal of Sex and Marital Therapy, 7,* 54–59.

Fromuth, M., & Burkhart, B. (1989). Long-term psychological correlates of childhood sexual abuse in two samples of college men. *Child Abuse and Neglect, 13,* 533–542.

Genuis, M., & Violato, C. (1991). *A stepwise discriminant analysis of sexually abused males: A retrospective study.* Manuscript submitted for publication.

Greenburg, N.H. (1979). The epidemiology of childhood sexual abuse. *Paediatric Annals, 8*(5), 289–299.

Lew, M. (1990). *Victims no longer: Men recovering from incest and other sexual abuse.* Mount Dora, FL: Kids Rights.

Meiselman, K. (1986). Males in heterosexual incest. In K. Meiselman (Ed.), *Incest: A psychological study of causes and effects* (pp. 292–322). San Francisco: Jossey-Bass.
Pierce, R., & Pierce, L. (1985). The sexually abused child: A comparison of male and female victims. *Child Abuse and Neglect, 9*, 191–199.
Reinhart, M. (1987). Sexually abused boys. *Child Abuse and Neglect, 11*, 229–235.
Risin, L., & Koss, M. (1987). The sexual abuse of boys: Prevalence and descriptive characteristics of childhood victimizations. *Journal of Interpersonal Violence, 2*, 309–323.
Spencer, M., & Dunklee, P. (1986). Sexual abuse of boys. *Pediatrics, 78*, 133–138.
Steele, B. (1986). Notes on the lasting effects of early child abuse throughout the life cycle. *Child Abuse and Neglect, 10*, 283–291.
Vander-Mey, B. (1988). The sexual victimization of male children: A review of previous research. *Child Abuse and Neglect, 12*, 61–72.
Violato, C., & Genuis, M. (1991). *Problems of research in male child sexual abuse: A review.* Calgary, AB: Department of Educational Psychology, The University of Calgary.

Journal of Child and Youth Care Special Issue Pages 7 – 21
 ISSN 0840-982X

Evaluable Models of Child Sexual Abuse Treatment Programs

Margaret Williams and Joe Hudson
Faculty of Social Work, The University of Calgary

Abstract: A study was conducted under the auspices of National Health and Welfare, Canada, to develop evaluable models of child sexual abuse treatment, education/prevention and investigation programs. This article outlines the study and describes the treatment model developed, together with indications of the ways in which the model may be used for evaluation purposes.

The past decade has witnessed increased awareness of the prevalence and impact of child sexual abuse, along with emphasis on the place of evaluation research in social service programs. In Canada, these two parallel thrusts led to formulating a federal evaluation strategy on Canadian child sexual abuse programs. The first stage of the strategy began in early 1987 and involved the compilation of a National Inventory of treatment, education/prevention and investigation programs focusing on child sexual abuse along with reviews of the research and evaluation literature. The research reviews generally found that child sexual abuse program outcomes are only rarely assessed. A primary reason for this is that programs are poorly conceptualized. Program structure and logic, process and outcome are not usually articulated in a way that would enable programs to be evaluated. Social welfare planners, policy makers and administrators are therefore not in a position to assume that clearly defined programs are in place to serve victims of child sexual abuse.

Evaluable program models must be established before existing programs can be evaluated. Consequently, the second stage of the federal evaluation strategy focused on a study to develop evaluable models of child sexual abuse treatment, education and investigation programs. This article briefly describes the study approach taken, along with the treatment program model developed, and ways in which the model might be used for evaluation purposes.

STUDY DESCRIPTION

Sampling Procedure

A purposive sampling procedure was used to select 17 treatment programs for study from those programs identified in the National Inventory. The eleven criteria used in making the purposive selection were:

1. Geographical Location: an attempt was made to select programs so that all geographical regions were represented.
2. Degree of Structure: programs that were better established with a greater degree of structure and formalization were preferentially selected.
3. Reputation: Programs selected were well known and respected in the field according to the views of experts canvassed.
4. Number of Program Components: since education/prevention and investigation programs were included in the study, multi-component programs were preferentially selected for purposes of research convenience and efficiency of data collection.
5. Program Size: programs serving fewer than 100 clients per year were arbitrarily designated as "small," those serving between 100 and 200 clients were designated as "medium-sized" while those serving more than 200 clients were designated as "large." The aim was to include a range of program sizes.
6. Administrative Auspices: both public and private agencies were included.
7. Program Focus: some programs focus only on services to victims or offenders or adult survivors, occasionally specifying age categories, such as adult offenders or victims no younger than six. While such programs were not excluded, preference was given to programs offering a broader ranger of services.
8. Type of Intervention: some programs provide only group therapy or only family therapy, or focus on a specific type of intervention. These programs were not excluded solely on this basis but an attempt was made to select therapy programs offering a wider range of interventive modes.
9. Specificity to Sexual Abuse: generic programs, which provide sexual abuse counselling as part of a general counselling service were excluded since the focus of the study was on programs dealing specifically with child sexual abuse.
10. Age of Program: programs which had been in operation for a longer period of time were preferentially selected.
11. Degree of Interest: since it was not feasible to conduct the study without the interest and cooperation of participating agencies, those programs expressing little interest were excluded from the sample.

Instrumentation

A data-collection instrument was designed to gather information on the 17 programs making up the sample. Three general areas were addressed: program structure and logic, program processes and program measurement.

1. Program Structure and Logic: program structure and logic encompasses the entire system whereby resources (inputs) are used to accomplish results by means of specific activities (processes). One of the purposes of the instrument was to secure, from program data, a structure and logic model in which inputs are linked to activities and activities are linked to anticipated, actual and unanticipated results.
2. Program Processes: a second purpose of the instrument was to develop/prepare a program process model; that is, a detailed specification of how clients enter, go through and come out of the component, including all decision points, decision criteria and decision makers.
3. Program Measurement Model: a third purpose of the instrument was to develop a measurement model; that is, a detailed description of how inputs, processes and results are measured in the program under study.

Description

Figure 1 is a schematic representation of the structure and logic of a child sexual abuse treatment model derived from data synthesized from 17 programs. This model presents key elements of program structure — inputs or resources, activities and associated subactivities and results — and a set of linking assumptions.

Certain resources or inputs are obviously necessary to enable programs to carry out their activities. In Figure 1, seven key types of resources are identified: program philosophy; organizational structure and context; funding/financial support; staff and volunteers; clients/ service users; referral sources and community resources.

The model also depicts a sets of activities necessary for a child sexual abuse treatment program and includes: client recruitment/intake; treatment planning; treatment intervention; and termination/discharge and follow-up. Activities can be categorized at various levels from the very general — operating a program — to the very specific — changing seating positions during family therapy. These activities form a logical progression from the general to the specific. For example, operating a program involves treatment intervention; treatment intervention involves implementing a treatment plan; a treatment plan may include family therapy; and one of the techniques used in family therapy may be changing seating positions. Because a general model cannot encompass every possible activity level, Figure 1 follows this progression only through three levels, from operating a program, to treatment intervention to implementing the treatment plan.

In a similar fashion, each activity and subactivity produces results and these also follow a logical progression. For example, changing seating position might contribute to a more appropriate family structure; an improved family structure contributes to a functional family system; a functional family system contributes to a healthy living situation for the child victim; and a healthy living situation means that abuse is less likely to reoccur. Again, because of the limitations of a general model, this progression of results from the potential (the reoccurrence of abuse is prevented) to the immediate (an appropriate family structure is achieved) is followed in Figure 1 only through the first three stages and is expressed in more general terms. That is, the overall program goal can only be reached if treatment goals are achieved, and treatment goals can only be achieved if the treatment plan is implemented.

The effectiveness of each activity in achieving its goal or intended result can be assessed at every stage. For example, if the activity is to fill out a referral form, one measure of effectiveness is how completely and accurately the form is filed out. On a different level, however, the purpose of filling out a referral form is not just to make marks on the paper; it is to gather information which will form the basis both for the intake decision and, later, for the treatment plan. Thus, a prior activity is involved — designing the intake form — and the measure of effectiveness here is whether a sufficient amount of useful information is requested to enable the intake decision to be made and the treatment plan to be initially conceived. If some information on the form is never used and additional information in some areas is always required, it is apparent that the form is not fully effective. In this way, measures or indicators of effectiveness are outlined for every activity.

DISCUSSION

Each of the 17 programs in the study sample expressed its overall program goals differently. However, there was sufficient commonality to allow a synthesis, leading to the emergence of two goals for child sexual abuse treatment programs: to minimize the likelihood of reabuse of the child victim; and to reduce the possible traumatic effects which family members may be experiencing as a result of the abuse. The treatment goals of the program are expected to be achieved through the four overall activities presented in Figure 1. The intended results of these activities should therefore sum to the intended results or goals of the program as a whole. The likelihood of reabuse of the child victim is minimized by effecting changes in both individual family members and the structure and dynamics of the family as a whole. Similarly, possible trauma may be minimized by effecting changes in individual attitudes and perceptions. These desired changes become the treatment goals outlined in Figure 1 as the results of the overall activities of planning and intervention.

Treatment goals are more likely to be achieved if the persons admitted to the program meet the eligibility criteria; that is, if the goal of the intake overall activity is achieved. One of the goals of the termination/discharge and follow-up overall activity is to ensure that treatment gains are maintained and the likelihood of reabuse continues to be minimal.

The activities and associated subactivities presented in Figure 1 will be discussed separately, with a focus on how each may be evaluated to provide useful information.

Client Recruitment/Intake. As shown in Figure 1, the goal or intended result of the overall intake process is that "a suitable number of clients with appropriate characteristics are admitted to the program in a timely manner." In other words, the program's caseload is maintained within a manageable range, its mandate is fulfilled, and clients likely to benefit from its services are admitted within a reasonable time period.

The two activity subcomponents identified in Figure 1 amount to: establishing and monitoring eligibility criteria; and establishing, implementing and monitoring intake and referral responsibilities. Of these, the first is a design activity while the second involves both design activities and activities which are more operational in nature. A design activity is defined as an activity which is not experienced by the client directly. It is a more singular activity, usually carried out at program inception and thereafter revised and monitored only as necessary. For example, the establishment of eligibility criteria and intake and referral procedures are design activities. Intake decisions based on these criteria and procedures, however, are made separately for each referral and are experienced directly by each potential client. In this way, implementing the procedures and making an intake decision are operational rather than design activities. For the sake of completeness, the model includes both kinds of activity.

The results of the two activity subcomponents are given in Figure 1 and are respectively: "the program has a clearly defined client population"; and "referrals and intakes are handled in an orderly manner and persons meeting program criteria are admitted." The results of these two activity subcomponents sum to the result of the overall activity. Evaluation of the recruitment/intake overall activity would therefore assess the degree to which the results of the subcomponent activities have been achieved; that is, the degree to which the program has a clearly defined client population, the extent to which referrals and intakes are handled in an orderly manner and the proportion of persons admitted to the program who meet eligibility criteria.

Clearly, however, these questions must first be operationalized. For example, what is meant by "a clearly defined client population" or "handled in an orderly manner"? The process of operationalization involves two steps: identifying the particular variables which best define the question; and deciding how those variables are to be measured. The second step, measurement, in itself comprises three parts: first deciding what the measurement is to be — for example, a head count or the score from a standard instrument; second, deciding by what process the measurement is to be made — who will make it, how, where and when; and third, deciding how the measurement is to be recorded so that it will be readily accessible and useful to program staff. The recording of measurements will not be discussed in this paper since the manual or computerized recording systems presently in use by child sexual abuse treatment programs are specific to individual programs. Work is being done to develop a more general computerized information system which will allow measurements to be recorded and accessed in such a way that they can be used by program staff to guide program activities in an ongoing manner.

Several variables can be used to describe "a clearly defined client population." For example, most program eligibility criteria include a residential qualification. Other criteria centre around client and family characteristics and history. Some programs may only deal with intrafamilial abuse or may not serve offenders or victims under a certain age, and so forth. The variables and measurements and measurement methods described in Table 1 are suggested to describe "a clearly defined client population."

Table 1

VARIABLE	MEASUREMENT	MEASUREMENT METHOD
Caseload range	Numerical range, from the minimum required by the program's mandate to the maximum that staff can accommodate.	Established at program's inception and revised periodically.
Present caseload	Numeric	Individual and total caseloads updated weekly by secretary.
Client characteristics	Place of residence Demographic information. Type, duration and frequency of abuse. Child welfare/legal status. Relationship of client to victim.	Filled out by worker on intake sheet according to information given by referral and other sources.
	Client and family history with regard to previous abusive or violent incidents, substance abuse and psychiatric disturbance.	Filled out by worker on intake sheet according to information given by referral and other sources.

In a similar way, variables can be identified to define what is meant by "referrals and intakes are handled in an orderly manner." For example, what is the maximum time that should elapse between receiving a referral and making the intake decision? Are decisions being made within this time period? Is information about the decision disseminated to other involved professionals and, if so, by whom, in what manner, and in what period of time? These variables are summarized in Table 2 as follows.

Table 2

VARIABLE	MEASUREMENT	MEASUREMENT METHOD
Time elapsed between date of referral and date of intake decision.	Number of days.	Completed by intake worker when decision is made.
Time elapsed between date of referral and date when client is first seen.	Number of days.	Completed by therapist after first session with client.
Time elapsed between date of intake decision and date when involved professional is informed (for each professional). Mode of contact.	Number of days. Case conference, telephone or letter.	Completed by therapist when professional has been informed.

Treatment Planning. The goal or intended result of treatment planning, as given in Figure 1, is "treatment interventions are rationally and explicitly linked to problem conditions and target goals." Before the target or treatment goals can be established, the problem conditions must be identified through an assessment procedure. Assessment serves the additional purpose of ensuring that persons finally admitted to the program meet the eligibility criteria and are likely to benefit from the offered services. The first activity subcomponent shown in Figure 1 under Treatment Planning therefore deals with assessment and the intended result reflects the dual purpose of the assessment procedure.

"Sufficient and useful information" refers to the need to define the client's problem in such a way that desired change can be written in the form of a clear treatment goal and an intervention package can be designed to achieve that goal. There will thus be an obvious and explicit link between the problem, the intervention and the intended result. The following variables are suggested to both define the problem and ensure the appropriateness of the client for the program. Measurements given in Table 3 refer to standardized instruments although many sexual abuse treatment programs use therapist interviews or in-house instruments in conjunction with, or instead of, standardized instruments.

Table 3

VARIABLE	MEASUREMENT	MEASUREMENT METHOD
Time elapsed between making intake decision and assessment result.	Time in days.	Completed by therapist when assessment has been done.
Personality characteristics.	MMPI PIC (children)	Results entered by therapist or psychologist.
Self-esteem	Coopersmith scales	Results entered by therapist or psychologist.
Family structure and dynamics.	FACES III (Olsen)	Results entered by therapist or psychologist.
Communication	Parent-Adolescent communication forms.	Results entered by therapist or psychologist.
Sexual satisfaction	Index of Sexual Satisfaction	Results entered by therapist or psychologist
Marital satisfaction	Index of Marital Satisfaction	Results entered by therapist or psychologist.
Anxiety	State Trait Anxiety Inventory Child Anxiety Scale	Results entered by therapist or psychologist.
Depression	Beck Children's Depression Inventory	Results entered by therapist or psychologist.
Family environment	Family Environment Scale (MOOS)	Results entered by therapist or psychologist.
Social/sexual history	Narrative description	Results entered by therapist or psychologist.

The second activity subcomponent under Treatment Planning is given in Figure 1 as "establish a service agreement." The service agreement clearly delineates the links between problem, intervention and treatment goal established as a result of the assessment. In addition, it sets out treatment conditions, including: expected time frames for the achievement of each goal; responsibilities of therapist and client; description of the place, time, duration and type of sessions to be conducted; confidentiality considerations, what information is to be shared with whom and when; specification of monitoring procedures, what procedures will be used by whom and when; and procedures to be followed if treatment conditions fail to be met. Since therapy cannot continue indefinitely, time frames will include an anticipated duration for the entire therapeutic process as well as time lines for individual goals. The description of therapy sessions will specify, for example, that the client is to be involved in individual, group and dyadic therapy concurrently at the times and locations arranged. The final clause will outline procedures to be followed if, for example, the client frequently misses appointments, exhibits inappropriate and unmanageable behaviour or fails to progress to a reasonable degree. In effect, the first clause will outline the criteria for planned termination while the last clause will outline the criteria for unplanned termination. These variables are all measured in a narrative format by the therapist and will not be presented in tabular form.

The intended result of establishing a service agreement, as outlined in Figure 1, is that the client, therapist and involved others have an explicit and accurate understanding about problems to be worked, goals to be achieved, treatment conditions and monitoring procedures. This result will only be achieved if the service agreement, as defined by the variables given above, is in written form and is shared with and agreed to by all persons involved.

Treatment Intervention. The intended result of treatment intervention, as stated in Figure 1, is that treatment goals are achieved. If a thorough service agreement has been prepared, based on complete and accurate information, it is reasonable to expect that treatment goals will be achieved by implementing the agreement, monitoring progress and making revisions as necessary. Some effort is often involved, however, in engaging the client in treatment, particularly when treatment is initiated before the abuse has been substantiated in court and treatment has not yet been mandated for all family members. It may also be necessary to provide supplementary services for some clients such as babysitting or transportation, advocate for such services as financial aid, or coordinate services such as drug/alcohol abuse or anger management counselling.

The result of the first activity subcomponent under Treatment Intervention, as given in Figure 1, is "clients acknowledge the need for change and are ready to work, and impediments and obstacles to treatment are removed/overcome." The variables necessary to define the degree to which impediments and obstacles to treatment are removed/overcome may merely be a list of services coordinated or provided, with the duration of each service and the time elapsed between identifying the need for the service and putting it into place. It is assumed, for example, that if lack of transportation proves an obstacle to treatment, providing the transportation will remove the obstacle. It is less easy to prove a measure of the degree to which clients acknowledge the need for change and are ready to work. An obvious indicator is the words used by the client in making the acknowledgement. A second indicator may be prompt and regular attendance at therapy sessions. A third, more subjective indicator may be client attitude as perceived by the therapist and recorded in case notes.

The second activity subcomponent under Treatment Intervention is "monitor and revise planned intervention." The intended result is "knowledge is obtained of relative goal achievement and plausible reasons for failure to achieve goal, and a revised treatment plan is formulated." Knowledge of relative goal achievement may involve the readministration of standardized or in-house instruments or merely a therapist's report on the client's perceived progress in specified areas. For example, one of the goals for the offender may be that he/she acknowledges responsibility for the abuse after four or fewer treatment sessions. If no acknowledgement is given, the intervention may be revised and a longer time allowed for the acknowledgement, or termination and referral to an alternate service may be preferred.

Termination/Discharge and Follow-up. Figure 1 shows the intended result of termination and follow-up activities to be "termination occurs in accordance with treatment plan and treatment gains are maintained." The first activity subcomponent presented in Figure 1 deals with termination itself and means simply that planned termination will occur when the criteria stipulated in the service agreement have been met. Criteria for planned termination will also have been outlined in the service agreement together with the procedures to be followed in both cases. A number of the 17 treatment programs included in the study indicated a varying backlog of inactive cases where no formal termination had occurred. Backlogs are problematic for caseload management and program planning and underscore the need for ongoing monitoring of client progress. Therapists need to move cases to formal closure so that available resources can be focused on clients who continue to cooperate with treatment.

The second and third activity subcomponents under termination/discharge and follow-up deal with the maintenance of treatment gains. For example, programs which provide short-term therapy regularly refer clients to other treatment programs after termination. Clients may continue to belong to a self-help group or supplementary services such as a parent aide may continue to be provided for a time. The result of the second activity subcomponent is given in Figure 1 as "additional services are provided relevant to client needs." Variables required to define this result are: a list of those services which the client and the therapist have mutually decided need to be provided, together with the probable duration of the service; a list of the resources which will provide the required services; and a description, for each service, of the procedure by which the provision and usefulness of the service will be monitored.

The third activity subcomponent deals with follow-up services and procedures. Of the 17 programs included in the study, none followed clients after termination in any systematic way although several had plans to institute follow-up procedures in the future. The results of failing to follow clients systematically are that those victims still at risk or experiencing difficulties due to the abuse in later years are not identified. Long-term program effectiveness therefore cannot be established. Suggested follow-up activities are:

1. Decide who will be responsible for carrying out follow-up activities, e.g., the client's former therapist or a staff member whose sole responsibility is follow-up.
2. Decide at what intervals contact will be made with the former client. Since some clients may need more frequent contact than others, this decision may have to be made separately for each client.
3. Decide how the follow-up contact will be made, e.g., a telephone call, a personal interview or a mailed questionnaire.
4. Decide what information needs to be gathered from the client in order: (a) to identify those clients who are in need of further services; and (b) to give an indication of the long-term effectiveness of the program.
5. Decide how this information is to be recorded and how it is to be used. If the information is compiled in a form that is readily accessible, it might be possible to create a feedback loop whereby indications as to the program's long-term effectiveness are used to improve some aspect of the program.
6. Where possible, provide the necessary services to those clients who have been identified as in need.
7. Decide responsibilities and procedures for monitoring and revising the follow-up process, e.g., if follow-up interviews by a client's former therapist are showing a tendency to become therapeutic interviews, it might be decided to designate one staff person to conduct follow-up interviews on a full-time basis.

SUMMARY

Figure 1 is a schematic representation of the structure and logic of a child sexual abuse treatment program. It was derived from information collected during a detailed study of the key elements and measurement practices of 17 sexual abuse treatment programs across Canada. This program structure and logic model presents key elements of program structure and the set of assumptions linking them. Key elements of program structure are presented as program inputs or resources, activities and associated subactivities and results.

The four overall program activities presented in Figure 1 are: recruitment/client intake; treatment planning; treatment intervention; and termination/discharge and follow-up. Each of these overall activities has an intended result or goal. Together, the goals of these overall activities comprise the goals of the treatment program as a whole. In a similar fashion, the goals of any set of activity subcomponents sum to the goal of the overall activity.

The program as a whole or any part of the program may be evaluated by assessing the degree to which the goals have been achieved. For example, the overall intake activity may be evaluated by assessing the degree to which a suitable number of clients with appropriate characteristics are admitted to the program. More specifically, eligibility criteria may be evaluated by assessing the degree to which the program has a clearly defined client population.

The degree to which a result has been achieved can only be measured if the result has been operationally defined; that is, variables must be identified which, when added together, will clearly and exhaustively define the result. For example, "a clearly defined client population" will include a residential qualification and certain individual and family characteristics. Once the variables have been defined, the next step is to measure them. The process of measurement comprises three parts: first, deciding what the measure is to be; second, deciding by what process the measurement is to be made; and third, deciding how the measurement is to be recorded so that it will be readily accessible and useful to program staff. This paper has presented variables, measurements and measurement methods for each of the overall and subcomponent activities identified in Figure 1.

FIGURE 1

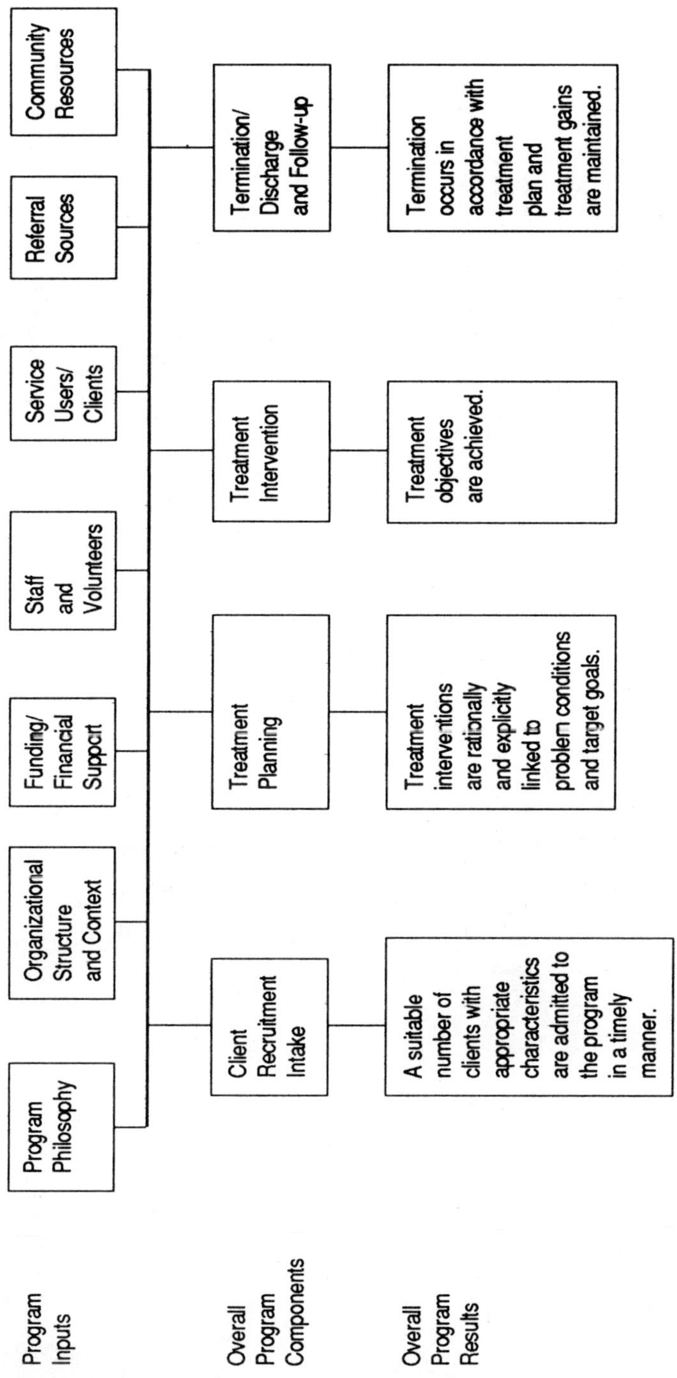
Program Inputs
Overall Program Components
Overall Program Results
Program Philosophy
Organizational Structure and Context
Funding/ Financial Support
Staff and Volunteers
Service Users/ Clients
Referral Sources
Community Resources
Client Recruitment Intake
Treatment Planning
Treatment Intervention
Termination/ Discharge and Follow-up
A suitable number of clients with appropriate characteristics are admitted to the program in a timely manner.
Treatment interventions are rationally and explicitly linked to problem conditions and target goals.
Treatment objectives are achieved.
Termination occurs in accordance with treatment plan and treatment gains are maintained.

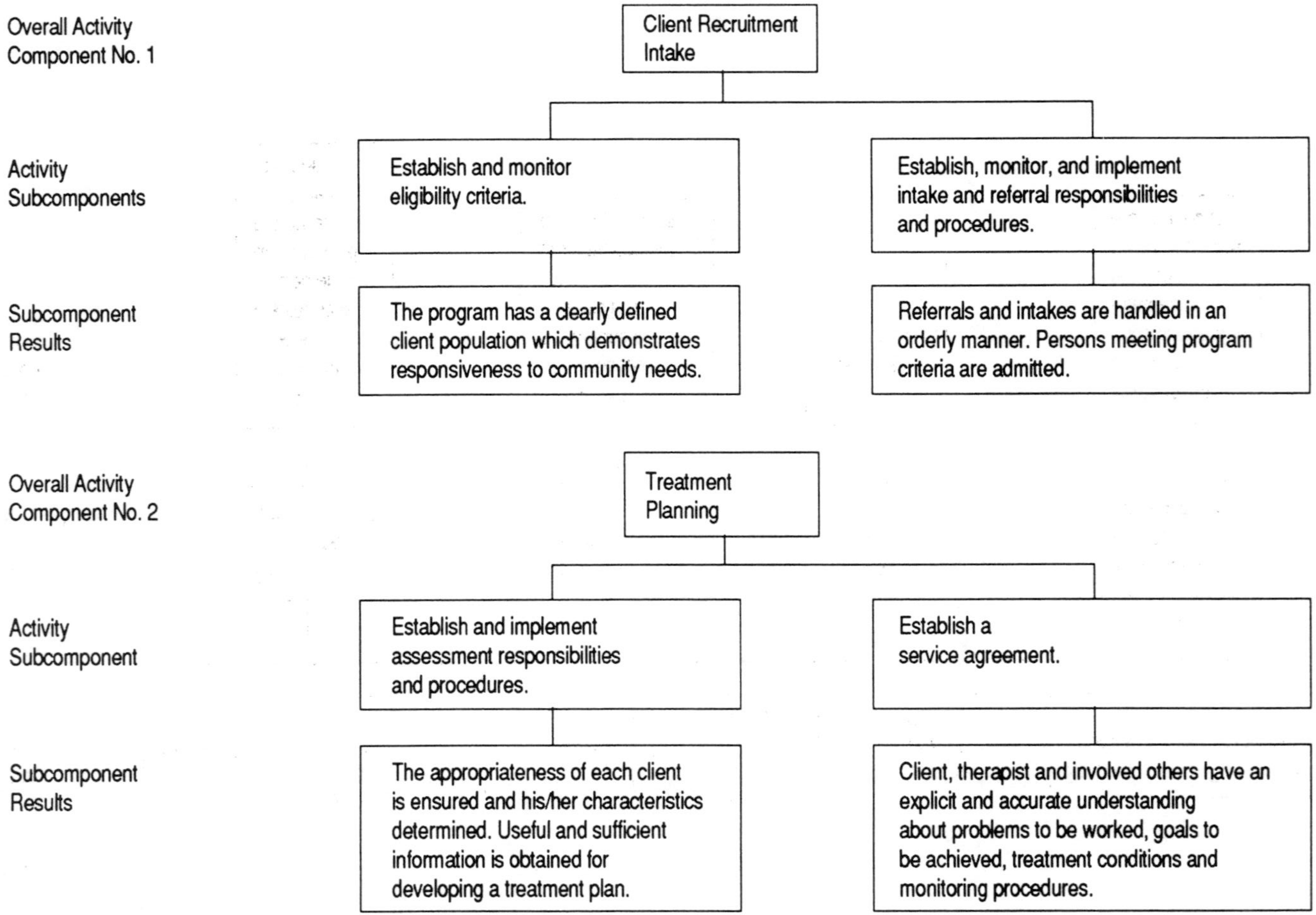
Overall Activity
Component No. 1
Client Recruitment
Intake
Activity
Subcomponents
Establish and monitor
eligibility criteria.
Establish, monitor, and implement
intake and referral responsibilities
and procedures.
Subcomponent
Results
The program has a clearly defined
client population which demonstrates
responsiveness to community needs.
Referrals and intakes are handled in an
orderly manner. Persons meeting program
criteria are admitted.
Overall Activity
Component No. 2
Treatment
Planning
Activity
Subcomponent
Establish and implement
assessment responsibilities
and procedures.
Establish a
service agreement.
Subcomponent
Results
The appropriateness of each client
is ensured and his/her characteristics
determined. Useful and sufficient
information is obtained for
developing a treatment plan.
Client, therapist and involved others have an
explicit and accurate understanding
about problems to be worked, goals to
be achieved, treatment conditions and
monitoring procedures.

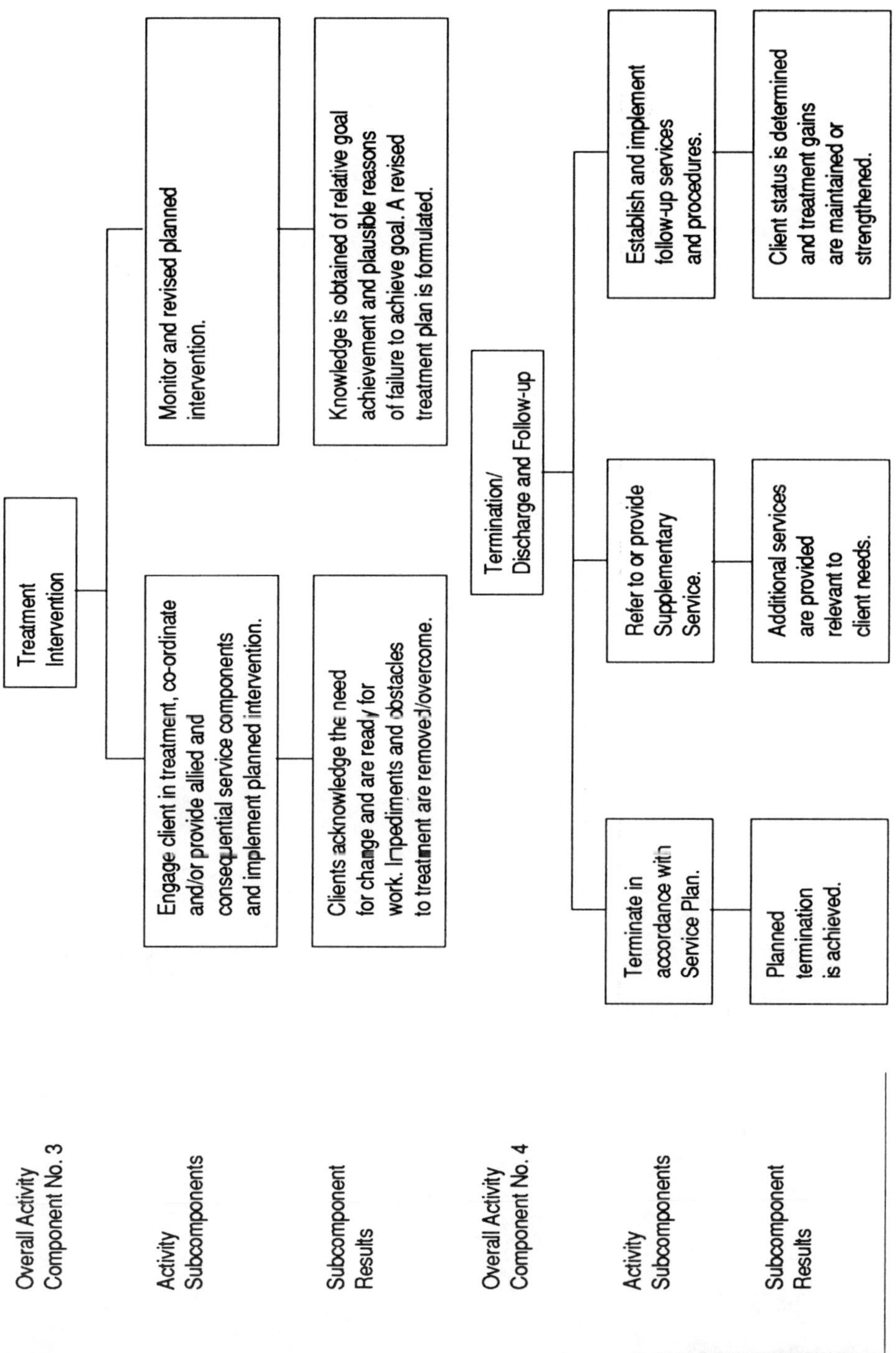
Overall Activity Component No. 3
Treatment Intervention
Activity Subcomponents
Engage client in treatment, co-ordinate and/or provide allied and consequential service components and implement planned intervention.
Monitor and revised planned intervention.
Subcomponent Results
Clients acknowledge the need for change and are ready for work. Impediments and obstacles to treatment are removed/overcome.
Knowledge is obtained of relative goal achievement and plausible reasons of failure to achieve goal. A revised treatment plan is formulated.
Overall Activity Component No. 4
Termination/ Discharge and Follow-up
Activity Subcomponents
Terminate in accordance with Service Plan.
Refer to or provide Supplementary Service.
Establish and implement follow-up services and procedures.
Subcomponent Results
Planned termination is achieved.
Additional services are provided relevant to client needs.
Client status is determined and treatment gains are maintained or strengthened.

Journal of Child and Youth Care Special Issue Pages 23 – 41
 ISSN 0840–982X

Child Sexual Abuse: A Range of Prevention Options

Leslie M. Tutty
Faculty of Social Work, The University of Calgary

Abstract: This paper presents a conceptual framework for organizing the wide variety of child sexual abuse prevention programs currently available. Examples of primary, secondary and tertiary prevention programs are described for each of Finkelhor's four preconditions considered necessary for sexual abuse to occur. An explanation of the preventative nature of each program is provided and its relevance assessed. Despite the number of different prevention formats, school-based child-directed programs have become the most commonly utilized. The current debate regarding this trend is delineated and a rationale for children as a key prevention target is presented.

Many prevention programs have been developed in the past decade in response to the realization that a number of children are at risk of sexual abuse and that the short- and long-term consequences of such abuse are severe (Browne & Finkelhor, 1986). These programs have been directed at a range of audiences: children, parents, teachers, and a host of mental health and child welfare professionals. It is now to the point where, if one speaks of sexual abuse prevention, some professionals will assume that one is speaking about school-based programs for children, others will envision programs to inform professionals about signs to detect child abuse, and still others will contemplate treatment programs for victims or adult survivors of abuse.

Clearly, the time has come to organize the variety of prevention programs into a framework so that one can easily identify the full range of options. Ordering these programs can aid in the assessment of which programs are most immediately useful, which may require more development before their implementation is possible, which deal directly with prevention and which suggest changes in society.

This paper presents such a framework, originally developed in 1987 (Tutty, 1990a). A variety of programs are described, some of which were designed specifically to prevent child sexual abuse, and others which, although they may have been developed for other purposes, have the potential to be preventative. The paper describes the recent debate surrounding the appropriateness of focusing on children, the most common abuse prevention audience, versus focusing on offenders. A

Table 1
Sexual Abuse Prevention Options: A Framework

Finkelhor's Preconditions	Primary Prevention	Secondary Prevention	Tertiary Prevention
1. Offender's Motivation	sex education	treatment for child victims who might become perpetrators	- aversion therapy - satiation - medication
2. Offender's Inhibitions	- public awareness advertisements - legal deterrents - ban child pornography	treatment for child victims who might become perpetrators - school-based programs stimulate disclosures	- cognitive restructuring - relapse prevention - covert sensitization
3. External Ilmpediments	- parent programs - target information to step families, single mothers	- programs for professionals for early identification, i.e., teachers, doctors	- treatment for parents of abused children after disclosure
4. Child's Resistance	- school-based programs - public awareness ads - self-esteem workshops - informal sources, eg., books, videos, T.V. shows - challenging traditional male-female stereotypes	- school-based programs stimulate disclosures - child telephone "hot lines" - routine questioning re: abuse in child welfare, mental health agencies - routine pediatric genital examination	- treatment for victims

rationale for supporting the continued use of child-focused prevention programs is presented.

THE FRAMEWORK

The following framework of the range of child sexual abuse prevention options utilizes Finkelhor's model of the preconditions necessary for sexual abuse to occur (1984):

1. A potential offender needed to have some motivation to abuse a child sexually.
2. The potential offender had to overcome internal inhibitions to act on that motivation.
3. The potential offender had to overcome external impediments to committing sexual abuse.
4. The potential offender or some other factor had to undermine or overcome a child's possible resistance to the sexual abuse (p. 54).

Prevention models which fit each of the four preconditions can be identified. If, as Finkelhor proposed, all four preconditions are necessary for abuse to occur, then intervention at any one of the preconditions constitutes prevention.

The first two preconditions refer to characteristics of the offender. The third and fourth preconditions, although stated in reference to the perpetrator, seem more amenable to prevention strategies since they refer to conditions often under the control of parents and children. For example, external impediments to the perpetrators' access to a child might refer to elements such as the presence of other people who could protect the child. Similarly, the fourth precondition might be influenced by teaching a child that she does not always have to do as adults demand if she feels uncomfortable.

One can identify programs in primary, secondary and tertiary prevention under each of these four preconditions (See Table 1).

Primary prevention refers to programs directed to a population before abuse occurs. Secondary prevention refers to efforts at both early intervention and treatment which would prevent long-term consequences. Tertiary prevention programs are those which intend to minimize the long-term consequences of children who have been abused (Caplan, 1964). Many professionals consider only primary prevention to be truly preventative (Albee & Gullotta, 1986), however, the following description of programs will, I believe, provide evidence that secondary and tertiary prevention programs are important in the prevention of child sexual abuse.

Precondition One. In the prevention of the first precondition, the motivation to sexually abuse a child, one can examine research on the formation of sexual identity. Authors, such as Groth (1978), have suggested that most child molesters are immature and have not had access to appropriate information regarding "normal" adult heterosexual activities. Some writers (Calderone, 1978; Gilgun & Gordon, 1985; Reibel, 1980; Cohn, 1986) believe that sex education and the use of appropriate erotica could prevent a fixation on children as sexual partners.

Victims who disclose abuse hopefully receive treatment, one goal of which is to prevent the victim from becoming a perpetrator in future. It is suspected that the incidence of male sexual abuse is significantly underestimated by disclosure statistics, since males are taught the importance of independence and self-sufficiency and are also less likely to disclose abuse because of implied homosexuality (Finkelhor, 1984). Male victims are therefore at even greater risk of abusing other victims. Groth and Burgess (1979) found that over one-third of 348 male offenders in their study admitted to having been sexually victimized as children. A recent follow-up study of 143 sexually abused children found that over 10 percent became adolescent perpetrators (Powell, 1988). It is not yet known why some victims become perpetrators and others do not; however, the development of secondary prevention programs to identify male victims (Sebold, 1987) by encouraging boys to disclose sexual abuse may, as Swift (1979) has suggested, be a vital link in the protection of future generations of children.

A tertiary prevention strategy aimed at identified perpetrators are behavior modification techniques to eliminate deviant sexual arousal, thereby preventing stimulation at the sight of children. Such techniques include aversive therapy (Kelly, 1982), and satiation (Walker, Bonner, & Kaufman, 1988). Medical approaches include the use of medications, such as Depo Provera, which act to temporarily reduce the sex drive of the individual. Although medication use is controversial, offenders often welcome such intervention as they feel at the mercy of their own sexual urges (Walker et al., 1988).

Precondition Two. To prevent the second precondition, overcoming internal inhibitions on the part of the offender, one can examine the effectiveness of legal deterrents and public awareness messages which clarify the illegality of sexually abusing children. Cohn (1986) proposes that the major responsibility for prevention should be placed on potential perpetrators rather than on the victims through the use of media messages such as "child sexual abuse is a crime," and "children get hurt when you sexually abuse them" (p. 561). Smith and Conte (1986) described another example: a billboard in downtown Seattle proclaimed "Using kids for prostitution is child abuse and it is a felony." This message was repeated on local television stations.

Child pornography victimizes children at two levels. First of all, children are shown pornography to convince them that the activities portrayed are fun, exciting, and an acceptable means of expressing affection (Tyler & Stone, 1985). Secondly, those children photographed in the materials were themselves exploited during the production of the pornographic materials. The availability of child pornography and the manner in which the children are portrayed as enjoying their experience also provides permission to the adult viewer to act on paedophiliac desires. Many countries, including Canada, have called for a ban of child pornography as a primary prevention strategy to address both the exploitation of further children and to provide a clear message to offenders about the illegality of sexually using children (Tyler & Stone, 1985).

Similar to the secondary prevention of the first precondition, programs aimed at treating victims, particularly young males, may prevent them from, in turn, victimizing other children. Early introduction to sexual activity often sexualizes otherwise normal relationships with peers. In one study comparing sexually abused to physically abused and to other children referred to a mental health clinic for reasons other than abuse (Gale, Thompson, Moran, & Sack, 1988) the symptom which most clearly differentiated the sexually abused group was inappropriate sexual behavior. Recent research (Cantwell, 1988, Cavanaugh Johnson, 1988) has described young victims introducing other children, often siblings (Smith & Israel, 1987), to the sexual behavior to which they were subjected. These young "perpetrators" ranged in age from four to thirteen. Intervention to prevent young victims from abusing other children has been previously suggested (Swift, 1979), but implemented in few programs, one exception being the program for child perpetrators described by Cavanaugh Johnson based in Los Angeles. One problem with this prevention approach remains the fact that most perpetrators, including child perpetrators, are male, and males are significantly less likely to report sexual abuse (Badgley, 1984; Briere, Evans, Runtz, & Wall, 1988), thereby not being available for treatment activities which could act as deterrents to future abuse. School-based sexual abuse prevention programs have been demonstrated to stimulate disclosures (Herring, 1984; Dawson, 1986) thus helping in the early identification of young victims/potential offenders, although their aim is more typically primary prevention.

Tertiary prevention of the second precondition is exemplified by treatment activities for offenders aimed at developing internal inhibitions rather than at changing the sexual orientation of the offender. The techniques are primarily behavioral and include cognitive restructuring, anger and stress management, "Relapse Prevention" (Pithers, Kashima, Cumming, & Beal, 1988), and covert sensitization (Walker et al.,1988). Most programs use combinations of these techniques in addition to more generally utilized behavioral treatments such as social skills training, assertiveness training and sex education. It is very difficult to evaluate the success of these programs because self-reported denial of further offenses cannot be taken at face value when admitting that treatment was ineffective would result in further criminal prosecution.

Precondition Three. Primary prevention efforts in this area, external impediments to committing sexual abuse, are typically addressed by parent education prevention programs and by alerting the community and key professional groups such as teachers, physicians, and day care providers to the risks and danger signals of sexual abuse. One impediment to the acknowledgment that sexual abuse is an important issue has been the fact that, until recently, it was regarded as a rare occurrence. Another common myth is that most perpetrators are strangers, when, in fact, over 80 percent of abuse is perpetrated by someone known to the child. Prevention programs that provide such information to parents and professionals alert them to be aware that sexual abuse most likely involves someone known to the victim.

Mothers, in particular, are thought to be critical in the protection of children from abuse. Finkelhor (1984) has put forth this view:

> Of course there has been criticism that mothers have been blamed too frequently for abuse. This criticism has some validity. . . . But findings related to the importance of mothers in protecting children appear too regularly to be dismissed as sexism. There is growing evidence that when mothers are incapacitated in some way, children are more vulnerable to abuse. (pp. 58–59)

Such circumstances as illness, death, divorce or psychosis of a mother can lead to children suffering abuse. Mothers who are physically or emotionally abused by their husbands may also be psychologically unavailable. In Herman's (1981) study of victims of father-daughter incest 55 percent of the mothers had periodic disabling illnesses for which they were hospitalized at times, or they lived as invalids at home. Since mothers are the parent most likely to attend parent education programs in child sexual abuse (Finkelhor & Araji, 1983), they are a logical audience for at-risk programs.

It has been suggested that secondary prevention efforts which address external impediments to sexual abuse could focus on several groups of mothers whose children have been identified as "high-risk" for sexual abuse. Recent research by Conte, Wolf, & Smith (1989) has illustrated the subtle and sophisticated behavior of offenders in both choosing their victims and in desensitizing them to touch through progressively more intimate contact. The knowledge that perpetrators pick vulnerable children, such as children whose parents are alcoholic or divorced, is useful, in that we may also identify these groups in order to provide information about the risk of abuse. The children of single parent mothers and step-families are five times more likely to be sexually abused according to Finkelhor (1984). Mothers who fit into these subgroups may benefit from special sexual abuse prevention programs.

Early identification of victims is thought to potentially short-cut the prolonged emotional impact on victims. Teachers can play an important role in such secondary prevention given the large amount of time in which they interact with children. Several evaluations (Volpe, 1981; Hazzard, 1984; McGrath, Cappelli, Wiseman, Khalil, & Allen, 1987; McIntyre, 1987; Kleemeier, Webb, Hazzard, & Pohl, 1988) suggest that teacher training programs effectively improve the ability of teachers to identify signs of possible abuse and to deal with disclosures.

An example of a tertiary prevention program which addresses the third precondition is treatment for parents whose children have been discovered to be victims of sexual abuse. Parents are likely to have very strong reactions to disclosures whether the perpetrator is a stranger or a family member. Dealing with their own feelings in separate sessions from their child, either through the support of a counselor (Sanford, 1980) or in a parents' group, for example, Parents United (Giarretto, 1981), may be beneficial. Many practitioners believe that a supportive parental stance is critical in helping a child recover from abuse (Sanford, 1980; Adams-Tucker, 1981).

Precondition Four. The fourth precondition is the major target for the prevention programs most commonly utilized today. School based sexual abuse prevention programs have become the mainstay of the prevention movement's efforts to respond to the alarming rates of sexual abuse of children. Various programs are directed towards children of all ages, in the hope that teaching them to recognize potentially abusive situations and what to do if touched inappropriately, will decrease the incidence of abuse and prompt early intervention for those who have been abused in the past.

Most school-based prevention programs cover the same core concepts. These include the distinction between "good," "bad," and "confusing" touches, the right to control what happens to one's body, and the right to say "no" if a child is not comfortable with what is happening. Often body parts are labelled in the hope that children can learn anatomically correct names, and would therefore have a vocabulary to describe abuse if it was occurring. Many programs discuss "secrets," emphasizing that it is important to tell a grown-up you trust if someone wants you to keep a secret that feels uncomfortable. Children are given permission to say "no" to adults, and if they are touched inappropriately they are told to get away if possible and to tell a trusted adult. Disclosing abuse is one of the most important concepts taught in the programs and is underscored by mentioning that if a child discloses and is not believed, that she should keep on telling until someone believes her. Finally, children are taught that even grown-ups they know (including family members) might touch them in a way they do not like and that, even in those cases, it is important to tell (Conte, Rosen, Saperstein, & Shermack, 1985).

Variations occur in the format of the programs (whether puppet show, play, or poster series) and the explicitness of the material (does the program mostly describe touching rather than sexual touching?). Some programs emphasize "stranger-danger" rather than explaining the possibility that a trusted grown-up could be abusive. The length of the programs varies (from one hour performances with no follow-up discussion, to extensive curricula). Some programs offer the children the opportunity to practise the implied skills (saying "no," identifying who one could tell if abuse occurs).

In addition to information about possible abusers and coercive tactics children are also told that if abuse occurs it is not their fault, but that it is always the adult's responsibility. Such responses address the "stigmatization" element of Finkelhor and Browne's traumatogenic responses to sexual abuse where children not only have to deal with their feelings about the abuse, but also with the expectation that others will blame or mistreat them for having been sexually victimized (1985). By encouraging children to disclose abuse, programs also attempt to shortcut the feeling of "powerlessness," another traumatogenic dynamic. This is important, as clearly the programs do not simply aim to prevent the assaultive incident, but to also prevent further trauma, as proposed by Finkelhor and Browne's model.

Review of the research on school-based programs suggests that elementary school-aged children learn the concepts taught in the programs (Tutty, 1990b; Wurtele, 1987). Importantly, many of the feared negative side-effects, such as worry and nightmares, have not occurred in response to the programs (Wurtele & Miller-Perrin, 1987; Nibert, Cooper, & Ford, 1989; Tutty, 1990c), while parents have noted positive effects such as children introducing the subject of abuse in conversation (Nibert et al., 1989). The research has, however, raised questions about whether preschoolers have the cognitive ability to understand the complexities of the major messages in sexual abuse prevention programs. A review of research studies with this age-group has yielded conflicting evidence (Tutty, 1990b).

One problem with sexual abuse prevention programs directed to children is that, although children learn the information, it is difficult to, and has not yet been demonstrated, that this knowledge may be utilized to actually prevent abuse.

In addition to programs which provide specific information to children about sexual abuse, several non-specific programs have been suggested as preventative. Self-esteem has been recognized as important in being able to say "no" to unwanted touch (Fryer, Kerns Kraiser, & Miyoshi, 1987). General programs with a focus on self-esteem seem to help children apply the skills learned in sexual abuse prevention programs more easily.

Many writers, especially feminists (Rush, 1980; Herman, 1981; Butler, 1986), believe that sexual assault has been "made possible by a deep-rooted value climate which allows males to regard females, and especially powerless females, as suitable objects for all kinds of exploitation" (Bagley, 1984). Similarly, but from a male point of view, Porter (1986) has suggested that young male victims of sexual abuse have been neglected because of differential sex-role expectations of males and females. Both positions suggest that education which promotes a non-sexist ideology, could have an impact upon the sexual exploitation of children of either sex (Maher, 1987).

Secondary prevention programs which address the fourth precondition include telephone "hot lines" (Pierce & Pierce, 1985; Ney, Johnston, & Herron, 1985) which are thought to provide a more comfortable way to ask for advice about possible abusive situations or to make a disclosure. Routine questioning regarding abuse in all mental health and child protection agencies would constitute another form of early identification. Medical doctors have suggested that routine history-taking with questions about past and current abuse, as well as pediatric screening of all children in the form of routine genital examinations (Cantwell, 1981; Seidel, Elvik, Berkowitz, & Day, 1986) would be helpful in the early identification of sexual abuse victims. Finally, as mentioned earlier, although children who have been abused are not considered the main audience for school-based prevention programs, nevertheless disclosures are often forthcoming. One study (Dolan, 1984) documented a significant increase in disclosures of abuse in one county, after the implementation of a prevention program, in comparison to another county with no program.

Examples of tertiary prevention for the fourth precondition include treatment for children who have been abused, mainly utilizing a variety of groups for victims (i.e., Gagliano, 1987), individual play therapy (Walker & Bolkovatz, 1988) and art therapy (Naitove, 1982) and family therapy (Friedman, 1988). Usually combinations of these treatments are offered (Anderson & Mayes, 1982; Trepper & Barrett, 1986) as a multi-modal approach is seen as necessary, particularly in cases of intrafamilial abuse.

In summary, if one is interested in the prevention of child sexual abuse there are numerous choices of interventions. In my opinion, each of the programs mentioned has merit. There has developed, however, a major emphasis on children as the most appropriate audience for prevention concepts. Since this choice has been contentious, the next section will describe some of the most common issues in the debate about on whom the focus of abuse prevention programs should fall.

THE CHOICE OF SCHOOL-BASED PREVENTION PROGRAMS

Overwhelmingly, school-based programs have become the format of choice for the prevention of child sexual abuse. In Canada, Dube, Heger, Johnson, and Hebert (1988) found that school-based prevention programs exist across the country. A recent survey in the United States found that over 25 percent of all public schools provided prevention for at least one grade level (Daro, 1988, p. 137). One clear advantage of school-based programs is that most address more than one prevention audience. As primary prevention they are directed towards children, parents, and teachers, and as secondary prevention, they encourage victims to disclose so that treatment may be forthcoming. For some victims, treatment may prevent their becoming perpetrators, while for other victims it may prevent the development of more serious sequelae to the sexual abuse such as post-traumatic stress syndrome (Krener, 1985).

Burns and Barber (1987) have suggested several reasons why schools provide an appropriate setting for teaching about sexual abuse. First of all, children spend a great deal of time at school. There is ongoing contact between teacher and children which enables teachers to detect changes in behavior or emotional or behavioral problems, some of which may be related to abuse. In most cases schools already have a functioning relationship with the families of their pupils. School personnel, including teachers and school counsellors, are therefore in a unique position to assist abused children (Paisley, 1987; Holmes, 1987; Meyers & Parsons, 1987), and in most provinces in Canada, professionals, including educators, have a legal responsibility to report suspected abuse (Burns & Barber, 1987). Schools are a natural environment for prevention programs, providing the opportunity to address entire populations of children with an approach which suits the purpose of the institution — an informational format (Bloom, 1981).

The fact that school-based programs focus on children, the "victims" of sexual abuse, has, as mentioned earlier, been contentious. Some authors question why we are "burdening our children" with the responsibility to stop abuse rather than placing responsibility where it belongs — on the offender (Cohn, 1986; Swift, 1979). Others feel uncomfortable with the sexual aspects of sexual abuse, fearing that providing children with information about sexuality will destroy their innocence. Finally, some question whether it should not be the responsibility of parents to teach such concepts to children, rather than that of the school system. These are appropriate concerns and require careful consideration.

Firstly, why do we not place more emphasis on the perpetrator through the forms of prevention discussed under the first two preconditions, such as media campaigns stressing the illegality of the abuse, sexual education for all children, and encouraging victims to disclose abuse? I think these strategies are all important and deserve implementation, but one would be naive to believe that solely utilizing programs for perpetrators would solve the problem of sexual abuse. Most perpetrators are aware that their activities are illegal, so only when children begin to disclose more easily and when courts prosecute sexual abusers more successfully, will the illegality of sexually abusing a child act as an effective deterrent.

Sexual offenders rarely ask for help to stop their sexual behavior (Groth, 1978) and when they do, it is usually only after they have been caught. It would seem that relying on treatment strategies to cure perpetrators, and thereby stop sexual abuse, is unrealistic.

Smith and Conte (1986) asked convicted child offenders whether a media message might have successfully prevented their offenses. The offenders reported that "a message would only make an impact *just before* or *just after* their *first* offense" (1986, p.2). Even if the perpetrators can be believed, this is a very narrow time-period in which to target prevention efforts, and, as the authors conclude, not a prevention tool which could be reasonably expected to stop a developing offender.

The one prevention strategy aimed at perpetrators which does have special merit is encouraging male victims to disclose, and, subsequently, provides treatment which is also preventive in nature. Of course, not all male victims will become perpetrators (Finkelhor, 1987), but statistics which suggest that a majority of sex offenders were themselves molested (Groth & Birnbaum, 1979) provide strong evidence for such the treatment of young victims as a prevention strategy in itself. School-based prevention programs are the most logical medium to encourage young male victims to disclose.

Secondly, why not simply encourage parents to talk to their children about sexual abuse? Finkelhor (1983) conducted research to find out in more detail what parents tell their children about sexual abuse. Interviews were conducted with 521 Boston parents screened for the presence of a child between age 6 to 14. Of this group only 29 percent claimed that they had talked to their children about sexual abuse directly, however, an additional 31 percent felt they had spoken to their children in a more indirect way about sexual abuse (mostly in terms of kidnapping and strangers). Even among the 29 percent who spoke more openly about sexual abuse, the fact that relatives and familiar adults are the persons most likely to molest children was a serious omission in the discussion (parents may not have been aware of this dynamic). The age at which parents were more apt to speak to their children, at about age nine, is late when one considers that this is approximately the average age for disclosures of abuse which has already taken place.

In regard to gender, "both sons and daughters were talked to (or perhaps we should say, ignored) in roughly equal proportions." (Finkelhor, 1983, p.6) Despite the fact that parents considered the subject of great concern, they also found it extremely difficult to discuss. Even topics such as suicide and sexual intercourse were rated as less difficult to broach with their children. Parents also tended to believe that their own child was at little risk. Considering that media attention has focused largely on the danger of strangers, perhaps it is not surprising that parents focus discussions with children on this topic. It may be that parents do not really understand that children are at more risk from familiar adults. Finkelhor's study did not test parental knowledge so it is not clear that all the parents who talked to their children about sexual abuse had accurate information. It would be valuable to update Finkelhor's research, especially given the increasing media focus on sexual abuse since 1982. His study does, however, clarify the fact that parents find sexual abuse a very difficult topic to discuss with their children.

Parent training programs may be helpful in encouraging parents to talk about sexual abuse, particularly by supplying models of what to say. Several evaluations of parent training programs were discovered in the literature. Duerr Berrick (1988), for example, evaluated one parent training program and found disappointing results. Only one-third of these parents of preschoolers took the opportunity to attend the program and the parents learned little about the prevalence of sexual abuse, indicators of abuse, or appropriate responses to disclosure.

Painter (1988) looked at how effectively parents responded to a prevention programs for preschoolers, but her design was more sophisticated, comparing the effects of two different, but readily available video programs, "Feeling Yes, Feeling No," and "Strong Kids, Safe Kids," and whether a discussion group conducted by a sexual abuse expert added to either video. She was able to randomly assign about 300 parents to six conditions: no treatment control, video 1, video 2, video 1 plus discussion, video 2 plus discussion, and a discussion with no video group. Her results showed that the discussion added significantly to parents' knowledge, attitudes, and potentially appropriate response in a hypothetical abuse situation. Interestingly, the "Feeling Yes, Feeling No" video was rated as superior since parents who saw this program ultimately felt more comfortable discussing sexual abuse with their children. Painter's findings thus suggest that once parents can be encouraged to attend a program, some formats may be more appropriate than others. Her research does not address how to motivate parents so that they will attend in the first place.

Some adults are concerned about exposing children to information about sexuality, although school-based programs have been most tactful in their descriptions of sexually sensitive topics (Finkelhor & Araji, 1983). Nonetheless, young children are more sexually knowledgeable than most adults think. Their family upbringing leads to the development of attitudes, knowledge, and rules about sexual behavior while they are still preschoolers (Stitt, 1980; Sgroi, Bunk, & Wabrek, 1988).

It has been a practical, but not necessarily an advantageous procedure to separate issues of sexuality from sexual abuse in school-based prevention programs. Children would be better served by learning information on human sexuality before learning about sexual abuse. No matter how sensitive and well-conceived, sexual abuse prevention programs still provide a negatively-framed view of sexuality; a "you have to be careful" mentality. While many prevention programs are provided to the early grades in elementary school, often classes in human sexuality are not presented until the later elementary grades. Although this is changing in some communities, fitting sexual abuse into a broader context of normal sexuality as well as self-esteem and caring for oneself emotionally, is, as yet, rarely offered.

Finally, why are some individuals so wary about providing children with the information and skills to protect themselves, such as those offered in school-based programs? Semantics are a key part of the argument. Critics complain about the "burden" and the "weight of responsibility" placed upon young children. Some even accuse prevention programs of "victim blaming," by making the child responsible for her own protection, an inappropriate use of the term, in my opinion. Supporters, in contrast, speak of "empowering" children and providing them with the knowledge they need to realistically cope in their world.

The dilemma has been usefully portrayed as "protection" versus "empowerment" (Butler, 1986), yet it seems to me that both ends of the spectrum are necessary. If children are taught effective ways to protect themselves not only will they be more self-sufficient, but their self-esteem will be enhanced. At the same time, parents and professionals must remain vigilant about the problem of child sexual abuse. Empowerment of children does not imply totally handing over the responsibility to protect them.

Further evaluation of school-based programs would help to clarify this issue. If it can be demonstrated that the programs can effectively teach children skills which are useful in avoiding sexual assault, without promoting increased anxiety or worry about positive, appropriate touch, then perhaps we can stop worrying about imposing unwanted responsibility on our children.

CONCLUSION

The opportunities for professionals and the public to increase their awareness of the dynamics of sexual abuse are many. The more we know about the problem, the more likely we are to recognize and to prevent further victimization of countless children. The implementation of school-based programs raises the possibility that the next generation of adults may know enough to provide informed protection for their children and that they will not be as unwilling to discuss sexuality and sexual abuse as our generation has been.

Nevertheless, other prevention options have important places in a multi-modal and concerted effort to prevent further victims of child sexual abuse. Unfortunately, they have not received the same support as school-based programs. For example, treatment for offenders and young victims is still not automatically forthcoming after abuse has been disclosed. Training for professionals, including social workers, teachers and doctors often does not include a mandatory course on child sexual abuse.

For new professionals wishing to jump on the bandwagon of sexual abuse prevention, there are still many opportunities to intervene: there is plenty of room and many novel, as well as familiar, directions in which to travel.

An earlier version of this paper was published as a chapter of a monograph, "A Critical Analysis of Child Sexual Abuse Prevention Programs," by the Centre for Social Welfare Studies, Wilfrid Laurier University, Waterloo, Ontario.

REFERENCES

Adams, C., & Fay, J. (1986). Parents as primary prevention educators. In M. Nelson & K. Clark (Eds.), *The educator's guide to preventing child sexual abuse.* Santa Cruz, CA: Network Publications.

Adams-Tucker, C. (1981). A socioclinical overview of 28 sex-abused children. *Child Abuse and Neglect, 5*, 361–367.

Albee, G., & Gulotta, T. (1986). Facts and fallacies about primary prevention. *Journal of Primary Prevention, 6*, 207–218.

Anderson, C., & Mayes, P. (1982). Treating family sexual abuse: The Humanistic approach. *Journal of Child Care, 1*, 31–45.

Badgley, R., Chairman. (1984). *Sexual offenses against children. Volume 1: Report of the Committee on Sexual Offenses Against Children and Youths.* Ottawa, ON: Ministry of Supply and Services.

Bagley, C. (1984). Mental health and the in-family sexual abuse of children and adolescents. *Canada's Mental Health, 32*, 17-23.

Bloom, M. (1981). *Primary prevention: The possible science.* Englewood Cliffs, NJ: Prentice Hall.

Briere, J., Evans, D., Runtz, M.M., & Wall, T. (1988). Symptomology in men who were molested as children: A comparison study. *American Journal of Orthopsychiatry, 53* (3), 457–461.

Browne, A., & Finkelhor, D. (1986). Impact of child sexual abuse: A review of the literature. *Psychological Bulletin, 99*, 66–77.

Burns, G., & Barber, P. (1987). The role of guidance personnel in the prevention of child abuse. *Canadian Journal of Counselling, 21* (1), 18–32.

Butler, S. (1986). Thinking about preventive education — A critical look. In M. Nelson & K. Clark (Eds.), *The educator's guide to preventing child sexual abuse.* Santa Cruz, CA: Network Publications.

Calderone, M. (1978). Is sex education preventative? In C. Qualls, J. Wincze & D. Barlow (Eds.), *The prevention of sexual disorders: Issues and approaches.* New York: Plenum Press.

Cantwell, H. (1981). Sexual abuse of children in Denver, 1979: Reviewed with implications for pediatric intervention and possible prevention. *Child Abuse & Neglect, 5*, 75–85.

Cantwell, H. (1988). Child sexual abuse: Very young perpetrators. *Child Abuse and Neglect, 12*, 579–582.

Caplan, G. (1964). *Principles of preventive psychiatry.* New York: Basic Books.

Cavanaugh Johnson, T. (1988). Child perpetrators — Children who molest other children: Preliminary findings. *Child Abuse and Neglect, 12*, 219–229.

Cohn, A. (1982). Stopping abuse before it occurs: Different solutions for different population groups. *Child Abuse and Neglect, 6*, 473–483.

Cohn, A. (1986). Preventing adults from becoming child molesters. *Child Abuse and Neglect, 10*, 559–562.

Conte, J., Rosen, C., Saperstein, L., & Shermack, R. (1985). An evaluation of a program to prevent the sexual victimization of young children. *Child Abuse and Neglect, 9*, 319–328.

Conte, J., Wolf, S., & Smith, T. (1989). What sexual offenders tell us about prevention strategies. *Child Abuse & Neglect, 13*, 293–301.

Daro, D. (1988). *Confronting child abuse.* New York: Free Press.

Dawson, R. (1986). *Program Report of the Oxford County Sexual Abuse Prevention Program.* Woodstock: Family and Children's Services of Oxford County.

Dolan, K. (1984). Evaluation of outcomes for reported cases of child sexual abuse in Texas. *Victimology, 9*, 383–397.

Duerr Berrick, J. (1988). Parental involvement in child abuse prevention training: What do they learn? *Child Abuse and Neglect, 12*, 543–553.

Dube, R., Heger, B., Johnson, E., & Hebert, M. (1988). *Child sexual abuse prevention: A guide to prevention programs and resources.* Montreal: Hôpital Sainte-Justine.

Finkelhor, D. (1983, August). *What parents tell their children about sexual abuse.* Presentation to the American Psychological Association. Anaheim, CA, August 1983.
Finkelhor, D. (1984). *Child sexual abuse: New research and theory.* New York: Free Press.
Finkelhor, D. (1986). Prevention: A review of programs and research. In D. Finkelhor (Ed.), *A sourcebook on child sexual abuse.* Beverly Hills, CA: Sage.
Finkelhor, D. (1987). The trauma of child sexual abuse: Two models. *Journal of Interpersonal Violence, 2* (4), 348–366.
Finkelhor, D., & Araji, S. (1983) *The prevention of child sexual abuse: A review of current approaches.* Paper presented at the American Orthopsychiatric Society, Toronto.
Finkelhor, D., & Browne, A. (1985). The traumatic impact of child sexual abuse: A conceptualization. *American Journal of Orthopsychiatry, 55,* 530–541.
Friedman, S. (1988). A family systems approach to treatment. In L. Walker (Ed.), *Handbook on sexual abuse of children: Assessment and treatment issues* (pp. 326–349). New York: Springer.
Fryer, G., Kerns Kraizer, S., & Miyoshi, T. (1987). Measuring actual reduction of risk to child abuse: A new approach. *Child Abuse and Neglect, 11,* 173–179.
Gale, J., Thompson, R., Moran, T., & Sack, W. (1988). Sexual abuse in young children: Its clinical presentation and characteristic patterns. *Child Abuse and Neglect, 12,* 163–170.
Gagliano, C. (1987). Group treatment for sexually abused girls. *Social Casework: The Journal of Contemporary Social Work, 67,* 102–108.
Garbarino, J. (1987). Children's response to a sexual abuse prevention program: A study of the *Spiderman* comic. *Child Abuse and Neglect, 11,* 143–148.
Giarretto, H. (1981). A comprehensive child sexual abuse treatment program. *Child Abuse & Neglect, 6,* 263–278.
Gilgun, J., & Gordon, S. (1985). Sex education and the prevention of child sexual abuse. *Journal of Sex Education and Therapy, 11,* 46–52.
Groth, A. (1978). Patterns of sexual assault against children and adolescents. In A. Burgess, A. Groth, L. Holmstrom & S. Sgroi. (Eds.), *Sexual assault of children and adolescents.* Lexington, MA: Lexington Books.
Groth, A., & Birnbaum, H. (1979). *Men who rape: The psychology of the offender.* New York: Plenum Press.
Groth, A., & Burgess, A. (1979). Sexual trauma in the life histories of rapists and child molesters. *Victimology, 4,* 10–16.
Hazzard, A. (1984). Training teachers to identify and intervene with abused children. *Journal of Child Psychology, 13,* 288–293.

Herman, J. (1981). *Father-daughter incest.* Cambridge: Harvard University Press.

Herring, B. (1984). *Preventive education program: An evaluation.* A report to the Metropolitan Toronto Special Committee on Child Abuse. Unpublished manuscript, Toronto.

Holmes, C. (1987). Prevention of child abuse: Possibilities for educational systems. *Special Services in the Schools, 3*, 139–153.

Kelly, R. (1982). Behavioral reorientation of pedophiliacs: Can it be done? *Clinical Psychology Review, 2*, 387–408.

Kercher, G., & McShane, M. (1984). The prevalence of child sexual abuse victimization in an adult sample of Texas residents. *Child Abuse & Neglect, 8*, 495–502.

Kleemeier, C., Webb, C., Hazzard, A., & Pohl, J. (1988). Child sexual abuse prevention: Evaluation of a teacher training model. *Child Abuse and Neglect, 12*, 555–561.

Krener, P. (1985). After incest: Secondary prevention? *Journal of the American Academy of Child Psychiatry, 24*, 231–234.

McGrath, P., Cappelli, M., Wiseman, D., Khalil, N., & Allan, B. (1987). Teacher awareness program on child abuse: A randomized controlled trial. *Child Abuse & Neglect, 11*, 125–132.

McIntyre, T. (1987). Teacher awareness of child abuse and neglect. *Child Abuse & Neglect, 11*, 133–135.

Maher, P. (1987). The school's proactive role in reducing levels of child abuse. In P. Maher (Ed.), *Child abuse: The educational perspective* (pp. 212–232). Oxford: Basil Blackwell.

Meyers, J., & Parsons, K. (1987). Prevention planning in the school system. In J. Hermalin & J. Morell (Eds.), *Prevention planning in mental health* (pp. 111–150). Newbury Park, CA: Sage.

Naitove, C. (1982). Arts therapy with sexually abused children. In S. Sgroi (Ed.), *Handbook of clinical intervention in child sexual abuse* (pp. 269–308). Lexington, MA: Lexington Books.

Ney, P., Johnston, I., & Herron, J. (1985). Social and legal ramifications of a child crisis line. *Child Abuse & Neglect, 9*, 47–55.

Nibert, D., Cooper, S., & Ford, J. (1989). Parents' observations of the effect of a sexual abuse prevention program on preschool children. *Child Welfare, 67* (5), 539–547.

Painter, S. (October 1988). *Impact of sexual abuse prevention materials — What works?* Presentation to the Institute for the Prevention of Child Abuse Conference, Toronto.

Paisley, P. (1987). Prevention of child abuse and neglect: A legislative response. *The School Counsellor, 34*, 226–229.

Pierce, R., & Pierce, L. (1985). Analysis of child sexual abuse hotline reports. *Child Abuse & Neglect, 9*, 37–45.

Pithers, W., Kashima, K., Cumming, G., & Beal, L. (1988). Relapse prevention: A method of enhancing maintenance of change in sex offenders. In A. Salter (Ed.), *Treating child sex offenders and victims: A practical guide* (pp. 84–207). Newbury Park, CA: Sage.

Porter, E. (1986). *Treating the young male victim of sexual assault: Issues & intervention strategies*. Syracuse, NY: Safer Society Press.

Powell, G. (1988). Child sexual abuse research: The implications for clinical practice. In G. Wyatt & G. Powell (Eds.), *Lasting effects of child sexual abuse* (pp. 271–281). Newbury Park, CA: Sage.

Riebel, J. (1980). Sexual abuse of children: A prevention strategy. In J. Sampson (Ed.), *Childhood and sexuality: Proceedings of the International Symposium* (pp. 688–693). Montreal: Editions Etudes Vivantes.

Rush, F. (1980). *The best-kept secret*. Englewood Cliffs, NJ: Prentice Hall.

Sanford, L. (1980). *The silent children: A book for parents about the prevention of child sexual abuse*. Garden City, NY: Anchor Press.

Sebold, J. (1987). Indicators of child sexual abuse in males. *Social Casework: The Journal of Contemporary Social Work, 67*, 75–80.

Seidel, J., Elvik, S., Berkowitz, C., & Day, C. (1986). Presentation and evaluation of sexual misuse in the emergency department. *Pediatric Emergency Care, 2* (3), 157–164.

Sgroi, S., Bunk, B., & Wabrek, C. (1988). Children's sexual behaviors and their relation to sexual abuse. In S. Sgroi (Ed.), *Vulnerable populations: Evaluation of treatment of sexually abused children and adult survivors. Volume 1* (pp. 1–24). Lexington, MA: Lexington Books.

Smith, T., & Conte, J. (1986). What can offenders teach us about prevention? *Preventing Sexual Abuse, 1* (2), 1–3.

Smith, H., & Israel, E. (1987). Sibling incest: A study of the dynamics of 25 cases. *Child Abuse and Neglect, 11*, 101–108.

Stitt, A. (1980). Sexually knowledgeable preschoolers and what we should do about them. In J. Samson (Ed.), *Childhood and Sexuality: Proceedings of the International Symposium*. Montreal: Editions Etudes Vivantes.

Swift, C. (1979). The prevention of sexual child abuse: Focus on the perpetrator. *Journal of Clinical Child Psychology, 8*, 133–136.

Trepper, T., & Barrett, M. (Eds.). (1986). *Treating incest: A multimodal systems approach*. New York: Haworth Press.

Tutty, L. (1990a). Preventing child sexual abuse: A review of current research and theory. In M. Rothery & G. Cameron (Eds.), *Child maltreatment: Expanding our concept of helping* (pp. 259–275). Hillsdale, NJ: Lawrence Erlbaum.

Tutty, L. (1990b). *A critical analysis of child sexual abuse prevention programs*. Waterloo, ON: Centre for Social Welfare Studies, Wilfrid Laurier University.

Tutty, L. (1990c). *The effectiveness of child abuse prevention programs: An evaluation of the Hamilton-Wentworth Child Abuse Prevention program, "Touching."* Waterloo, ON: Centre for Social Welfare Studies, Wilfrid Laurier University.

Tyler, R., & Stone, L. (1985). Child pornography: Perpetuating the sexual victimization of children. *Child Abuse & Neglect, 9*, 313–318.

Volpe, R. (1981). The development and evaluation of a training program for school-based professionals dealing with child abuse. *Child Abuse & Neglect, 5*, 103–110.

Walker, C., Bonner, B., & Kaufman, K. (1988). *The physically and sexually abused child: Evaluation and treatment issues*. New York: Springer.

Walker, L., & Bolkovatz, M. (1988). Play therapy with children who have experienced sexual assault. In L. Walker (Ed.), *Handbook on sexual abuse of children: Assessment and treatment issues* (pp. 249–269). New York: Springer.

Wurtele, S. (1987). School-based sexual abuse prevention programs: A review. *Child Abuse and Neglect, 11*, 483–495.

Wurtele, S., & Miller-Perrin, C. (1987). An evaluation of side effects associated with participation in a child sexual abuse prevention program. *Journal of School Health, 57*, 228–231.

Journal of Child and Youth Care Special Issue Pages 43 – 52

Characteristics of 60 Children and Adolescents Who Have a History of Sexual Assault Against Others: Evidence From a Controlled Study

Christopher Bagley and Daria Shewchuk-Dann
Faculty of Social Work, The University of Calgary

Abstract: Sixty individuals aged 9 to 17 in two residential treatment centres for severely disturbed children and adolescents were identified as having a history of sexual assault against others. Comparison with 320 age and sex-matched controls indicated that the sexually assaultive individuals displayed the following statistically significant differences: more self-concept problems, more hyperactivity or restlessness, more aggression towards father, more anxiety, more depression, more histories of substance abuse, more running from home, more encopresis, more fire-setting, and more early-onset neurological conditions or illnesses. The sexually assaultive youth displayed significantly fewer acts which fell in the range of traditional delinquency (physical assault and theft). The sexually assaultive youth tended to come from intact, 'hothouse' families which often manifested gross pathology, including physical and sexual assault of the child.

Research reviewed by Bagley and King (1990), including data from the national Canadian survey of child sexual abuse (Bagley & Thurston, 1989) indicates that a high proportion — perhaps as many as 20 percent — of sexual assaults on children are committed by adolescents. Moreover, a minority of these adolescents go on to become chronic sexual offenders against children, adolescents or adult women and if untreated may have many hundreds of victims during their lifetime (Bagley & Thurston, 1989). Obviously, the identification and treatment of adolescent sex offenders could be highly cost effective. Yet programs in this area are not well developed, and indeed much basic knowledge about the nature and motivation of adolescents who offend sexually is lacking (Bagley & Thomlison, 1991).

Existing studies do, however, indicate that being a victim of child sexual assault significantly increases the risk of becoming an offender (Burgess, Hartman, & McCormack, 1987); many adolescents who are sexually assaulted experience rape by other adolescents (Ageton, 1983; Burgess, 1985). While sexually assaultive behaviour may be normative in some adolescent subcultures, other adolescent sexual offenders have backgrounds of personal pathology and family disruption (Fehrenbach, Smith, Monastersky, & Deisher, 1986; Koss, Gidycz, & Wisniewzki, 1987).

Studies also show that the large majority of detected adolescent offenders are male (Fehrenbach et al., 1986; Groth & Laredo, 1981); adolescent offenders present challenges to treatment systems, but these challenges are not insuperable (Groth & Laredo, 1981; Johnson & Shrier, 1987; Ryan, Lane, Davis, & Isaac, 1987; Smets & Cebula, 1987; Thomas & Rogers, 1983).

METHODS: SURVEY OF ADOLESCENTS IN RESIDENTIAL TREATMENT

The data on which the present study is based come from a file review of 670 children and adolescents admitted to two residential treatment centres in the period 1979 to 1987. A standardized method of deriving information from files was devised, and there was agreement between the four individuals who abstracted data from this and other studies of the residential populations (Bagley & Young, 1990). The two centres, located in Southern Alberta, provide treatment for severely disturbed children and adolescents.

During the period in which these young people were referred, sexually assaultive behaviour was never the primary reason for treatment, and the file reviewers often had to read through a mountain of documents before finding the report of sexual assault by the child or adolescent. Sometimes such activity was usually dismissed as part of a normal developmental process, and it must be borne in mind that because of possible biases in recording and reporting such assaults, we may have included some individuals in the "non-assaultive" group who had in fact engaged in sexual assault. To the extent that this is the case, the results reported below are conservative estimates of the differences between the groups.

In the present study only data from files of male children were analyzed, since the number of female sexual abusers are too small to warrant inclusion. The subjects consisted of those youths whose files mentioned sexually assaultive behaviours. The pool of potential controls consisted of all the other children in the treatment centre who were male and who fell into the same age range as the abusers, namely nine through sixteen. The files were reviewed, coded and scanned for any sign of sexually abusive behaviour. When a file did note sexually abusive behaviour, it was further reviewed, and along with the completion of the coding schedule, a brief description of the child and the family or any other pertinent information that had not been requested on the standardized coding schedule was noted. In addition, files of approximately five control subjects of the same age were selected for review, on a random basis. "Sexual abuse" involved any sexual action or assault which was judged to be contrary to the Criminal Code of Canada.

We did not seek to interview any of the children or their families. Such a course was procedurally and ethically too difficult, but it must be recognized that personal interviews could well provide additional clinical information. Approximately 12 percent of male children in the two facilities engaged in sexually abusive behaviour of some kind.

There were some problems in collecting data as most files were not organized in a systematic fashion. It was only with extensive reading that we were able to uncover that the child had in fact sexually assaulted somebody. Frequently this was mentioned in just a paragraph or two, without comment, or with a conclusion that this is normal development or that a child will "outgrow" this behaviour. In a number of cases however, problems were longstanding, the child's initial contact with child welfare personnel having started as early as three years of age, continuing on a regular basis thereafter. Some of these files were inordinately thick, requiring an experienced file reader to spend up to four or five hours plodding through massive amounts of data.

What was most interesting was the lack of any focus in the therapeutic programs on the child having sexually assaulted others, or continuing sexual assaults. Both centres stressed a behavioural approach, and addressed current problem behaviours, rather than their early cause.

The reliability of coding was assessed through a comparison of the ratings of four raters for fifty cases. There was an 85 percent concordance in rating ($p < .000$). between each of the four raters. Disagreements usually related to judgments about missing data, or placement of ratings in adjacent categories.

QUALITATIVE DESCRIPTIONS

Prior to describing the results of the statistical data, we wish to present characteristic vignettes of some of the individuals whose files were reviewed:

Case One is a 13-year-old boy who was removed from the foster home of his aunt and uncle after he had sexually assaulted his two-year-old female cousin and his six-year-old male cousin. Prior to having been placed in this foster home, he had had "sexual experience with other children." This statement was simply noted in the file with no accompanying information.

Case Two is a boy who was apprehended at the age of two and subsequently placed in various foster placements up to age 14. He had been drinking alcohol since the age of seven, exhibiting anger, suicidal behaviour, and fighting. The file noted that he had "strong and unusual attachment to his brother," again with no further explanation. At the time of admission, he had had a girlfriend for approximately one year, and had recently engaged in intercourse with his two-year-old cousin while babysitting.

Case Three was a child who had engaged in "incidents with dogs," "beating younger children," "collecting female panties," "bestiality," and was described as having a fascination with fire. The file also noted that there was sexual conflict and assault in family of origin. When he was a young child he consistently urinated on the floor and then played in his urine. His sexual relations with animals including dogs and horses were addressed by transferring him to new places of residence.

Case Four was a child who was first referred to child welfare authorities when he was three, due to his "sexually inappropriate behaviour." At age five the child and his mother were asked to leave the Women's Emergency Shelter due to the boy's sexual involvement with other children. The file had consistent records of child welfare consultations because of sexually inappropriate behaviour by either this boy, or his parents. At the time of our reading the file, the boy was 11 years old and was exhibiting "inappropriate sexual behaviour" towards staff and peers in the treatment centre. He had informed staff that he sexually enjoyed watching people get hurt and was particularly sexually excited by the thought of stepping on the heads of young children, or beating women about the breasts. One assessment done of this boy showed that there was a problem with "sex in family." Both the boy's father and mother had been convicted of sexual assault on other children in the family.

None of the above children were receiving any treatment for their sexually abusive behaviours. Furthermore, although some had been assessed following this sexually abusive behaviour, none of the assessments indicated that the assaultive behaviour was in itself serious or should be further followed up by treatment specific to the behaviour. We found further, that of the assessments that were conducted, none reviewed all of the sexual behaviours that were often noted earlier in the file. Rather, it appeared that a specific incident of sexual behaviour was dealt with separately from any other incident, if it was dealt with at all.

STATISTICAL FINDINGS

Table 1 shows the results of the comparison between individuals with a recorded history of sexual abuse, and controls. Sexual abusers were significantly more likely to come from intact families, that is, families where the original two parents stayed together. The families of the abusive youth experienced more severe marital tension than intact families in the control group; mothers of abusers had more mental health problems requiring treatment; fathers of abusers had more mental health problems requiring treatment, and were also slightly more likely to drink alcohol excessively. Unstable families (defined by several male figures, and/or frequent desertions by the father figure) had higher prevalence in the control group.

Prior to being admitted to the treatment centres, the sexually assaultive youths who had separated from biological families were more frequently resident in a group home, than in a foster home. They were more likely to have experienced severe physical abuse and/or sexual abuse both within the home and outside of the home, and to be the recipients of harsh discipline. These youth came primarily from families who could be classified as blue collar or lower white collar. Chronically unemployed or welfare parents were more typical of the control group than the sexually assaultive group.

The sexually assaultive youths exhibited behavioural profiles which had many statistically significant differences from controls. They showed marked self-concept problems, more hyperactivity or restlessness, more aggression towards father, more anxiety, depression, substance abuse, running away from home, and neurological conditions than the control group. These youthful sexual abusers were also more likely to engage in serious fire-setting, and to have been encopretic than the control group. They were, however, less likely to be destructive of possessions and/or property outside their home, and less likely to be grade-retarded with no specific learning disabilities.

General or specific learning disorders emerged as important variables, occurring more frequently in the abusive group. Also statistically significant was the fact that the parents of the sexually assaultive youths were more frequently over-ambitious for their child, and unduly critical of the child's poor school grades. These sexually assaultive youths also had significantly more impairment of sight or hearing, and significantly more neurological conditions of early onset.

A principal component analysis of the data was carried out (table not shown) and indicated that the sexually assaultive youths had health problems that began earlier (before the age of three) than the control group's health problems. It also showed that their behaviour could be clustered around the following behavioural profiles: neurological problems, hyperactivity, aggression towards father, encopresis, and fire-setting. Their personal adjustment, more frequently than that of the control group, showed the following symptoms: depression, anxiety, poor self-concept, and suicidal ideas and behaviours. However, the control group demonstrated more aggressive behaviour towards peer groups and siblings. The control group was also significantly more destructive of possessions and/or property than the sexually abusive group.

DISCUSSION

In the process of this analysis, it was apparent that the treatment programs in place in the two institutions studied, only rarely addressed sexual abuse as a problem during the period of file reviews. In many instances, no mention could be found on file anywhere as to whether an enquiry had been made to determine if these children had themselves been victims of abuse at some point. This highlights both the lack of awareness of sexual abuse issues, and the possibility of conservative bias in this research. It is clear, however, that the assaultive youth are much more likely to have been sexually or physically assaulted themselves than controls.

These young assaultive male children tend to come from families that are maritally intact but with much stress present and parents who are often unstable or mentally ill. We would speculate that when parents stay together in adverse conditions, they are not necessarily providing an environment conducive to the mental health of their children. It is suspected too that the sexual abuse experienced by these boys has major etiological significance in the development of their own sexually abusive behaviour.

Sexually assaultive youths were also more likely to be in institutional group homes prior to admission to the treatment centres. Presumably these children could not be contained in a conventional foster home. The sexually assaultive youths were considered less aggressive towards others (particularly peers) and less destructive of possessions and property than other youths in the treatment program, but nevertheless what was usually addressed in treatment was their delinquency. The fire-setting behaviour observed in a third of the assaultive youth usually involved their place of residence, rather than the community.

Although this research was conducted within treatment centres for severely disturbed children, the statistically significant results can cautiously be generalized to adolescent sexual abusers who are not in treatment centres. This study concurs with much of what is known from past research. It also brings new data to light, particularly with regards to the early neurological and health problems, and the families of these youths. The results also highlight the apparent importance of health and learning disorders. A most interesting new finding is that sexual abuse is related to family dysfunction and arises within the context of family pathology within intact homes. It is further interesting that the youth are primarily from lower middle class or blue collar homes, rather than from disorganized or disrupted families.

Table 1
Sixty Males Aged 9 to 17 Who Were Sexually Assaultive Compared With 322 Age and Sex-matched Controls: Both Groups Resident in Treatment Centres in Southern Alberta, 1978–1987

Variable	Significance of Chi-squared	Cramer's V or Phi	Trend	
Age on admission	.252	.07	SA: Con:	14.2 years 14.4 years
Intact family with two parents (adoptive or biological)	.000	.25	SA: Con:	76% 51%
Severe marital tension in family in 3 years prior to admission	.020	.19	SA: Con:	36% 25%

Variable	Significance of Chi-squared	Cramer's V or Phi	Trend
Child had single parent at time of admission	.039	.15	SA: 13% Con: 23%
Stepfather in home at time of admission	.145	.07	SA: 22% Con: 28%
Stepmother in home at time of admission	.943	.02	SA: 7% Con: 5%
Mother has had mental health problems needing treatment	.026	.15	SA: 17% Con: 9%
Father (where present) has had mental health problem needing treatment	.000	.37	SA: 28% Con: 15%
Mother suffers from severe drinking problem	.828	.04	SA: 6% Con: 4%
Father (where present) suffers from severe drinking problem	.052	.09	SA: 17% Con: 12%
Unstable family (several male figures, or frequent desertions by father and frequent conflict with partner)	.000	.30	SA: 20% Con: 41%
Resident in group home prior to admission	.000	.24	SA: 57% Con: 35%
Native Indian, Inuit or Metis	.325	.07	SA: 23% Con: 19%
Evidence of severe physical abuse of child prior to admission	.000	.24	SA: 28% Con: 13%
Evidence of sexual abuse of child in the home prior to admission	.000	.55	SA: 54% Con: 5%
Evidence of sexual abuse of child outside the home prior to admission	.000	.48	SA: 31% Con: 3%
Parent(s) chronically unemployed/on welfare	.014	.19	SA: 1% Con: 19%
Parent(s) blue collar or lower white collar	.012	.21	SA: 61% Con: 49%
Number of siblings 3+	.007	.26	SA: 25% Con: 35%
Evidence of inconsistent discipline, veering from harsh to lax	.050	.11	SA: 32% Con: 25
Evidence of consistently harsh discipline in home	.035	.16	SA: 22% Con: 13%
Parent(s) judged to be over-ambitious for child/unduly critical of poor school grades	.001	.19	SA: 14% Con: 3%
Death of father	.910	.02	SA: 3% Con: 4%

Variable	Significance of Chi-squared	Cramer's V or Phi	Trend
Death of mother	.854	.08	SA: 0% Con: 2%
Severe behavioural problems emerged by age seven	.000	.36	SA: 16% Con: 32%
Marked self-concept problems	.005	.20	SA: 65% Con: 52%
Very poor relationship with peers (aggression/withdrawal)	.345	.03	SA: 67% Con: 64%
General or specific learning disorder	.000	.41	SA: 58% Con: 22%
Grade retarded, but has IQ in normal range, and no specific learning problems	.000	.27	SA: 16% Con: 40%
Marked hyperactivity or restlessness, now or in past	.000	.29	SA: 35% Con: 23%
Destructive of possessions and/or property	.000	.30	SA: 32% Con: 46%
Marked aggression to mother	.053	.09	SA: 4% Con: 9%
Marked aggression to father	.000	.30	SA: 49% Con: 25%
Marked aggression to siblings	.182	.13	SA: 18% Con: 21%
Marked symptoms of anxiety	.004	.22	SA: 35% Con: 20%
Marked depressive symptoms	.011	.12	SA: 23% Con: 15%
History of deliberate self-harm on at least one occasion	.047	.09	SA: 28% Con: 23%
History of drug, alcohol or solvent use to excess	.012	.18	SA: 20% Con: 14%
Has run from home at least twice	.015	.19	SA: 34% Con: 28%
Has been convicted of at least two criminal offences	.215	.06	SA: 28% Con: 24%
Has a significant neurological condition (e.g., fits, hemiplegia)	.000	.20	SA: 24% Con: 10%
Has a significant impairment of sight or hearing	.000	.20	SA: 20% Con: 8%
Has been markedly encopretic	.000	.23	SA: 18% Con: 3%

Variable	Significance of Chi-squared	Cramer's V or Phi	Trend
Has engaged in serious fire-setting	.000	.40	SA: 33% Con: 8%
Child was adopted	.342	.04	SA: 18% Con: 17%
Problems of health including over-activity, neurological and other problems before age 3	.000	.39	SA: 36% Con: 14%
Component of behaviour: Runs; aggression to peers; destructive; delinquent — score above 50th percentile	.050	.08	SA: 46% Con: 52%
Component of behaviour: neurological problems; hyperactivity; aggression to parent(s); encopresis; fire-setting — score above 50th percentile	.000	.52	SA: 80% Con: 41%
Component of behaviour: depression; anxiety; poor self-concept; suicidal ideas and behaviour — score above 50th percentile	.000	.38	SA: 64% Con: 46%

Note: Calculation of Chi-square is based on tables with a varied number of cells, and the whole range of variation is not displayed in the above table. Phi is a correlation coefficient based on Chi-squared for a 2x2 table; Cramer's V is a correlation coefficient derived from Chi-squared for a 2xN table. For definitions and formulae see Nie, Hull, Jenkins, Steinbrenner, and Bent (1975) for description of the SPSS package, which was used for the analysis of the above data.

SA = Sexual Abusers. Con = Control Subjects.
Cases with missing data were excluded in the above analysis, so the N is variable in each comparison.
For method of establishing "component of behaviour" profiles, see Bagley and Young (1990)

REFERENCES

Ageton, S. (1983). *Sexual assault among adolescents.* Toronto: Lexington Books.

Bagley, C., & King, L. (1990). *Child sexual abuse: The search for healing.* New York: Tavistock/Routledge.

Bagley, C., & Thomlison, R. (Eds.). (1991). *Child sexual abuse: Critical perspectives on prevention intervention, and treatment.* Toronto: Wall and Emerson.

Bagley, C., & Thurston, W. (1989). *Preventing child sexual abuse: Reviews and research.* University of Calgary: Rehabilitation and Health Monographs, No. 18.

Bagley, C., & Young, L. (1990). Taxonomy and treatment: The role of the scientist practitioner in child and youth care. In J. Anglin (Ed.), *Perspectives in professional child and youth care* (pp. 318–329). New York: Haworth Press.
Burgess, A. (1985). Sexual victimization of adolescents. In A.W. Burgess (Ed.), *Rape and sexual assault: A research handbook* (pp. 123–138). New York: Garland Publishing.
Burgess, A., Hartman, C., & McCormack, A. (1987). Abused to abuser: Antecedents of socially deviant behaviors. *American Journal of Psychiatry, 144*, 1431–1436.
Dann, D. (1987). *Youthful sexual abusers.* Unpublished master's thesis. The University of Calgary, Calgary, AB.
Fehrenbach, P., Smith, W., Monastersky, C., & Deisher, R. (1986). Adolescent sexual offenders: Offender and offense characteristics. *American Journal of Orthopsychiatry, 56*, 225–233.
Groth, A., & Laredo, C. (1981). Juvenile sexual offenders: Guidelines for assessment. *International Journal of Offender Therapy and Comparative Criminology, 25*, 31–39.
Johnson, R., & Shrier, D. (1987). Past sexual victimization by females of male patients in an adolescent medicine clinic population. *American Journal of Psychiatry, 144*, 650–652.
Koss, M., Gidycz, C., & Wisniewzki, N. (1987). The scope of rape: incidence and prevalence of sexual aggression in a national sample of higher education students. *Journal of Consulting and Clinical Psychology, 55*, 162–170.
Nie, N., Hull, C., Jenkins, J., Steinbrenner, K., & Bent, D. (1974). *Statistical package for the social sciences.* New York: McGraw Hill.
Ryan, G., Lane, S., Davis, J., & Isaac, C. (1987). Juvenile sex offenders: Development and correction. *Child Abuse and Neglect, 11*, 385–395.
Smets, A., & Cebula, C. (1987). A group treatment program for adolescent sex offenders: Five steps toward resolution. *Child Abuse and Neglect, 11*, 247–254.
Thomas, J., & Rogers, C. (1983). A treatment program for intrafamily juvenile sexual offenders. In J.G. Greer & I.R. Stuart (Eds.), *The sexual aggressor: Current perspectives on treatment* (pp. 127–143). New York: Van Nostrand.

JOURNAL OF CHILD AND YOUTH CARE SPECIAL ISSUE PAGES 53 – 63
 ISSN 0840–982X

CHILD SEXUAL ABUSE AND POLICE DISPOSITION: A CANADIAN STUDY

MICHAEL STEPHENS, RICHARD M. GRINNELL, JR.,
BARBARA THOMLISON, AND JUDY KRYSIK
FACULTY OF SOCIAL WORK, THE UNIVERSITY OF CALGARY

Abstract: This research note presents timely Canadian-based data on police disposition in cases of child sexual abuse. The data is compared and contrasted with recently published American data. The information was compiled from the files of an Alberta Social Service region. The study represents 147 confirmed cases of child sexual abuse. Specific variables examined were: perpetrator characteristics, the nature of the perpetrated offence, and the relationship of perpetrator characteristics and perpetrated behaviour to the resulting police disposition.

Child sexual abuse is the fastest growing form of reported child abuse (Finkelhor, 1983). In a six-year reporting period from 1976 to 1982 there was an increase in the number of reported cases of child sexual abuse across the United States from 1,975 to 22,918 (Russell & Trainor, 1984). In Canada, the Ontario Child Abuse Register for 1989 reported 1,448 cases of child abuse of which 1,109 were identified as child sexual abuse, a 500 percent increase over nine years (Shoalts, 1991). It is estimated that 100,000 children are sexually abused each year, yet the sexual abuse of children is the least reported category of criminal activity in proportion to its occurrence (Deitz & Craft, 1980). Research on the phenomenon of child sexual abuse has proliferated human service literature, resulting in increased public interest and concern (e.g., Finkelhor, 1983; Howes, 1986; Sgroi, 1982).

Despite voluminous literature dealing with child sexual abuse, the focus of available literature is predominantly on victims (e.g., Erickson, Walbek, & Seely, 1988; Russell, 1983; Finkelhor, 1980). As the rate of reporting child sexual abuse has increased, however, so has discussion regarding the abusive occurrence and prosecution of the offender (e.g., Baumann, Kasper, & Alford, 1984; Berliner & Conte, 1981; Graves & Sgroi, 1982). A dramatic increase in confinement of child sexual offenders has been reported in the United States over the past 10 years (Baumann et al., 1984).

The appropriateness of the justice system in dealing with victims of child sexual abuse and those who abuse them is a controversial issue.

Attitudes toward child sexual abuse may be influenced by the abusive activities that occur (Wilk & McCarthy, 1986). For example, one incident of fondling is generally tolerated more than multiple events of sexual intercourse (Finkelhor, 1983).

The purpose of the present study is to contribute to research findings regarding the perpetrator, the abusive occurrence, and resulting police disposition in cases of child sexual abuse.

METHODS

In Canada, child welfare is a provincially-legislated responsibility. In Alberta, *The Province of Alberta Child Welfare Act* was passed by the Alberta Legislature on 31 May 1984, and proclaimed on 1 July 1985. This Act forms the basis for child welfare intervention in Alberta. The Ministry which administers the Child Welfare legislation for the Province is Alberta Family and Social Services. Any allegation of child sexual abuse must be referred to Alberta Family and Social Services for investigation purposes.

The delivery of child welfare services in Alberta occurs through a decentralized system located in six geographic regions. This study was carried out in one of Alberta's largest regions which includes a large metropolitan city and the surrounding rural territory. Five geographic offices offered an investigation/intake program within the region.

Operational Definition

To be consistent with the study's setting, we adopted the operational definition of child sexual abuse as legislated by the Province of Alberta Child Welfare Act:

> A child is sexually abused if the child is inappropriately exposed or subjected to sexual contact, activity, or behaviour. Section 1(3) (c) p. 6.

Criteria for Sample Inclusion

Three criteria had to be satisfied in order for a child sexual abuse case to be included in the study. First, cases alleging child sexual abuse had to be referred to Alberta Social Services during the 1985 calendar year. The abuse itself did not have to occur in 1985, but must have been referred for investigation between 1 January 1985 and 31 December 1985.

The location to which the child sexual abuse was reported was the focus of the second criterion. To be included in this study the referral had to be made to the specified Region mentioned above. The second criteria was met if the referral was actually investigated by a child welfare worker within the Region under study.

The third criterion to be considered was assessment. To be included in the study, the investigating social worker was required to have assessed that child sexual abuse had indeed occurred.

The sample was therefore defined as: all cases of alleged child sexual abuse referred to Alberta Social Services in 1985; investigated by a child welfare worker within the identified Region; and in which the alleged sexual abuse was assessed as actually having occurred.

Sample

Having defined the sample by the above three criteria, the next step was to gather an inventory of all child welfare files. The study initially identified a preliminary group of 539 alleged victims who met the first two criteria. These 539 files were then reviewed to screen out those that did not meet the third criterion. This process identified 191 cases in which the investigating social workers concluded that child sexual abuse had occurred. Of the 191 child sexual abuse cases a total of 147 contained data on police disposition, while 44 cases had missing data. It is these 147 victims that form the final sample for this study.

Reliability and Validity

A data-gathering instrument was designed based upon a review of professional literature on child sexual abuse. Three employees of Alberta Social Services tested the instrument to affirm its content validity. Upon completion of this process, additions, modifications, and deletions were made in format and operational definitions of the instrument in order to increase validity.

A test for interrater reliability rendered an error rate of less than one percent. Twenty percent of all files (109) included in this study were randomly checked for reliability of data collection. Seven errors were present in a total of 9,146 responses. Where there was error (disagreement between the principal data gatherer and the person checking reliability) the files were rechecked and corrections were made.

RESULTS

Three separate variables are highlighted in this study. The dependent variable of the study is disposition following police investigation. Following investigation a disposition is made by the police, to either charge or not to charge the alleged perpetrator. The independent variables, perpetrator characteristics, and sexual offence are delineated into affiliated sub-variables and are reported as they relate to resulting police disposition.

Disposition

It is a policy of Alberta Social Services to adopt the "Giarretto Model" in the investigation phase of alleged child sexual abuse (Giarretto, 1976). A major precept of the Giarretto Model is to have the police involved in the investigation, and when possible, to charge the perpetrator with a criminal code offence.

The disposition of police investigation was used as the dependent variable in this study. Of the 147 perpetrators, 55 (37%) were charged and 92 (63%) were not charged (see Table 1). Wide variation in the use of criminal action in cases of child sexual abuse has also been reported across the United States (Finkelhor, 1983). Nevada, for example, reports that 43 percent of child sexual abuse cases have some criminal justice action. In Arkansas, criminal justice action occurs in less than 10 percent of child sexual abuse cases. Nationwide, 24 percent of all cases report the use of criminal action. Ideally, the true outcome variable could be the ultimate decision made in a court of law as the number of cases actually coming to trial, or ending in a conviction, are only a fraction of the percentage charged.

Table 1
Distribution of Sample by Disposition

Disposition	Number	Percent
Charged	55	37.4
Not Charged	92	62.6
Totals	147	100

The Perpetrator

There are many issues to be considered when examining the perpetrator in child sexual abuse. This section considers five perpetrator related sub-variables: relationship to the victim, perpetrator's gender, acknowledgement by the perpetrator of committing child sexual abuse, previous history of abuse as a perpetrator, and mean age at the onset of abusive behaviour.

The first sub-variable studied was the relationship of the victim to the perpetrator. Relationship to the perpetrator can be further broken down into two categories: intrafamilial or extrafamilial. For the purposes of this study, intrafamilial child sexual abuse occurred when there was a blood or legal familial relationship between the victim and the perpetrator. Extrafamilial child sexual abuse occurred when there was no blood or legal familial relationship between the victim and the perpetrator.

Summit (1980) reported that the large majority of perpetrators came from the victim's family. This study also identified intrafamilial child sexual abuse as predominant. In 47 percent of all reported cases the perpetrator was the individual in the father role. In addition, once all intrafamilial relationships were accounted for, 73 percent of child sexual abuse victims were either related to the perpetrator by blood or legal ties. The remaining 27 percent of perpetrators were not related to the victims.

Sixteen mutually exclusive categories are presented for the nominal level independent variable relationship. To determine if each relationship was correlated with police disposition a simple bivariate Pearson's product-moment correlation coefficient (r) was calculated. There were

Table 2
Distribution and Correlations Between Perpetrator Subvariables and Disposition

VARIABLE	Number Referred	Number Charged	Percent Charged	*r*
Relationship				
Natural Father	35	15	43	.06
Natural Mother	3	0	0	.11
Male Sibling	13	5	39	-.01
Step-Father	17	7	41	.03
Step-Male Sibling	1	1	100	-.11
Adoptive Father	3	2	67	.09
Uncle	9	2	22	.08
Male Cousin	6	1	17	.09
Grandfather	5	2	40	-.01
Significant Other	18	7	39	-.01
Peer	1	0	0	.06
Male Babysitter	11	4	36	.01
Male Careprovider	3	3	100	.19[b]
Common-Law Father	13	6	46	.06
Live-in Boyfriend	4	0	0	.13
Step-Grandfather	2	0	0	.09
Other Related	3	0	0	-.11
TOTALS	147	55	37	
Perpetrator's Gender				-.11
Male	144	55	38	
Female	3	0	0	
TOTALS	147	55	37	
Acknowledgement				.19[b]
Yes	44	22	50	
No	45	14	31	
TOTALS	89	36	40	
Previous History				.16
Yes	72	33	46	
No	8	3	38	
TOTALS	80	36	45	
Variable	Mean	*SD*	*n*	*t*
Age at Intake	29.9	13.2	106	1.87

b Statistically significant at .05, two-tailed test

extremely weak associations between all of the 16 relationships and disposition. The correlations ranged from .01 to .19. The bivariate correlation analysis supports the hypothesis that the relationship variables were not individually substantively related to police disposition.

The second sub-variable concerning the perpetrator was gender. There is an abundance of literature which indicates that males predominate in the commission of child sexual abuse (Finkelhor & Hotaling, 1984). This study's findings are clearly consistent with the literature in that 98 percent of the perpetrators were male. Finkelhor (1983) reported that only seven percent of female perpetrators are referred for criminal action. The results of bivariate analysis on the variable gender are not meaningful due to the small number of female perpetrators in this study.

The third variable considered was acknowledgement by the perpetrator of committing child sexual abuse. Since the perpetrators of child sexual abuse have everything to lose if children's stories are believed, it is more likely that they will deny the occurrence (Faller, 1984). Berliner and Conte (1981) suggest that the majority of offenders will plead guilty to the original charge when that charge does not carry a mandatory prison sentence, or in cases of incest in which a high social stigma is attached. Confessions of guilt appear to have a bearing on police disposition. There is a statistically significant but weak correlation (.19) between acknowledgement and disposition. The probability of being charged increases with acknowledgement of the child sexual abuse by the perpetrator.

Finkelhor (1983) identified a criminal record to be one of the single best predictors of resulting criminal action. Seventy-two (90%) of the perpetrators had a previous history of abuse (i.e., physical, sexual, or emotional) as perpetrators. Eight (10%) had no previous history as perpetrators. However, bivariate analysis does not support a relationship between previous criminal history and subsequent criminal action in this study.

A study by Pierce and Pierce (1985) reports the mean perpetrator age to be 34 years. The mean age of the perpetrator (male and female combined) in this study at the onset of abuse is 29.9 years — four years younger than the U.S. data. A Student's t-test was calculated to determine if there was a difference between the mean ages of those charged, as opposed to those not charged. The mean age of perpetrators who were not charged was 27.9. The mean age of perpetrators at the time of reporting for the charged group was 32.7. Although the charged group had a higher average age the difference was not statistically significant.

The Sexual Offense

The second variable that plays an important role in the study of child sexual abuse is the sexual offence. Five sub-variables related to the sexual offence were considered: location where the child sexual abuse took place, the primary sexual act, the person upon whom the activity was performed, frequency of occurrence, and duration of the abuse.

Table 3
Distribution and Correlations Between Perpetrator Subvariables and Disposition

VARIABLE	Number Referred	Number Charged	Percent Charged	*r*
Location				
Victim's Home	97	38	39	.10
Perpetrator's Home	23	4	17	-.18 b
Car	1	0	0	-.07
Public Place	4	3	75	.14
Other	7	3	43	.03
TOTALS	132	48	36	
Type of Activity				-.11
Exhibitionism	6	4	67	.14 b
Exposure/Adult Sex	2	1	50	.04
Voyeurism	1	0	0	-.06
Attempt Intercourse	9	4	44	.05
Fondle Breasts	8	2	25	-.05
Fondle Genitalia	50	14	28	-.11
Cunnilingus	3	1	33	-.01
Fellatio	4	2	50	.06
Anal Penetration				
Penile	3	2	67	.10
Digital	2	0	0	-.09
Penile Attempt	3	1	33	-.01
Vaginal Penetration				
Penile	23	11	48	.12
Digital	6	2	33	-.01
Other	4	1	25	-.04
Dry Intercourse	2	0	0	-.09
Kissing	2	0	0	-.09
Not Classifiable	6	2	33	-.01
Prostitution	1	0	0	-.06
TOTALS	135	47	35	
Recipient				
Victim	122	42	34	-.00
Perpetrator	8	4	50	.08
Other	2	1	50	.04
Both	4	0	0	-.14
	45	14	31	
TOTALS	136	47	35	

b Statistically significant at .05, two-tailed test

Table 3 (Continued)

VARIABLE	Number Referred	Number Charged	Percent Charged	*r*
Frequency				
Single	30	4	13	-.26 a
Multiple	98	43	44	.26 a
TOTALS	128	47	37	
Frequency				
Single	30	4	13	-.33 a
Less than 10	30	11	37	-.08
10 and More	40	23	58	.33 a
TOTALS	100	38	38	
Variable	Mean	*SD*	*n*	*t*
Duration of Abuse	19.5 mths	27.5	103	2.34

a Statistically significant .01, two-tailed test
b Statistically significant .05, two-tailed test

Since children have a need for safety and shelter, the location in which the perpetrator had access to the victim would be a significant factor should the child sexual abuse occur where safety is assumed (Showers, Farber, Joseph, Oshins, & Johnson, 1983). In this study, location was categorized by five mutually exclusive and exhaustive elements. Seventy-three percent of the child sexual abuse cases occurred in the victim's home. A bivariate analysis revealed no support for the hypothesis that police disposition is related to the location that the child abuse took place.

The second sub-variable regarding the occurrence is the primary sexual act. Berliner and Conte (1981) reported that 64 percent of the time the primary abusive act was fondling of genitalia. This study also reports that fondling was the sexual act that occurred most frequently (43%). Furthermore, Baumann et al. (1984) found that penetration occurred in less than one-third of child sexual abuse cases. This analysis found that anal or vaginal penetration took place in 30 percent of the child sexual abuse cases — consistent with the U.S. data.

A simple bivariate analysis was conducted for each type of activity and disposition. Correlation coefficients ranged from .01 to .14. Bivariate correlation analyses revealed that the type of activity involved in the child sexual abuse was not individually related to police disposition on a significant level. Also related to the type of activity is the question of upon whom the sexual act was performed. The most frequent occurrence (83%) found the victim as recipient of the sexual act. Bivariate analysis reveals extremely weak correlations between individual recipient categories and police disposition.

Frequency of occurrence in child sexual abuse has been given due attention in the literature (Finkelhor, 1983). The difference between a single occurrence and multiple occurrences is an important consideration in victim treatment and perpetrator disposition. Berliner and Conte (1981) have reported that the majority of cases (66%) include multiple occurrences. In contrast, they found that only 17 percent of the cases consisted of a single incident of abuse. This study was consistent with the above mentioned data. Multiple occurrences were present in 77 percent of the cases, as opposed to 23 percent reporting single occurrences.

Bivariate analysis revealed two statistically significant relationships between frequency and disposition. A multiple occurrence, and a frequency of ten or more offenses was moderately related to the likelihood of charges being laid.

The fifth sub-variable to be considered in regard to occurrence is the duration of abuse. Studies indicate large numbers of child sexual abuse situations continue for years prior to the victim's disclosure to a person in authority. Again this study was congruent with the literature. The mean duration of abuse for males and females combined was almost two years (19.5 months). Duration of abuse and resulting police disposition were not significantly related in this analysis.

IMPLICATIONS

Perpetrator sub-variables produced no strong bivariate relationships with disposition. The Giarretto Model adhered to by Alberta Social Services requires that the perpetrator be charged. Yet, only 50 percent of those perpetrators who acknowledged being involved in child sexual abuse were charged. Thus, despite recommendations to Crown prosecutors that criminal prosecutions be undertaken, this was not always done.

A disturbing statistic is that a total of 72 perpetrators, had a previous history as a perpetrator with a different victim. Of these 72 perpetrators only 33 were charged. Again, the policy maker should take note of this statistic in evaluating the difficulties of policy implementation in this area.

It is within the component of independent variables known as the occurrence variables where the study yields results that are a strong predictor of disposition. In cases where the child sexual abuse occurred greater then ten times, 57 percent of the perpetrators were charged. In cases of a single occurrence only 13 percent were charged.

The social work educator must emphasize to all professionals involved in the investigation of child sexual abuse that there is emotional damage done even when the child sexual abuse occurs on a single occasion. The decision to charge also varies with the type of sexual offence. Charges were laid by the Crown in only 27 percent of cases involving fondling, and for incidents of anal penetration, charges were laid in 66 percent of the cases. The definition of child sexual abuse legislated by Alberta Social Services does not rank frequency and types of activities from least damaging to most. For the practitioner, this demands an examination of attitude regarding tolerance of the type of activity and frequency.

The similarity of Canadian data to that from the United States have implications for further service development. The United States has a proliferation of information concerning child sexual abuse. Treatment programs, policy makers, and social workers could benefit greatly from the experience and expertise developed across the states; however, further study is necessary to validate and track the apparent similarities.

SUMMARY

In summary, this research has presented timely Canadian-based data on police disposition in cases of child sexual abuse. The information was compiled from the files of one Alberta Social Service region. Specific variables described were: characteristics of the perpetrator, details pertaining to the sexually abusive occurrence, and resulting police disposition.

This type of analysis is necessary to monitor trends, examine current policies and practices, and to guide the development and implementation of focused-intervention strategies. The findings of this Canadian-based study have proven to be generally consistent with those reported in the growing body of North American literature in the area of child sexual abuse.

REFERENCES

Alberta Social Services. (1984). *Province of Alberta Child Welfare Act.* Edmonton, AB: Queen's Printer.

Baumann, R.C., Kasper, J.C., & Alford, J.M. (1984). The child sex abusers. *Corrective and Social Psychiatry. 30*, 76–81.

Berliner, L., & Conte, J.R. (1981). Sexual abuse of children: Implications for practice. *Social Casework, 62*, 601–606.

Dietz, C.A., & Craft, J.L. (1980). Family dynamics of incest: A new perspective. *Social Casework, 61*, 602–609.

Erickson, W.D., Walbek, N.H., & Seely, R.K. (1988). Behavior patterns of child molesters. *Archives of Sexual Behavior, 7*, 77–86.

Faller, K.C. (1984). Is the victim of child sexual abuse telling the truth? *Child Abuse and Neglect, 8*, 473–481.

Finkelhor, D. (1980). Risk factors in the sexual victimization of children. *Child Abuse and Neglect, 4*, 265–273.
Finkelhor, D. (1983). Removing the child — prosecuting the offender in cases of sexual abuse: Evidence from the national reporting system for child abuse and neglect. *Child Abuse and Neglect, 7*, 195–205.
Finkelhor, D., & Hotaling, G.T. (1984). Sexual abuse in the national incidence study of child abuse and neglect: An appraisal. *Child Abuse and Neglect, 8*, 23–33.
Giarretto, H. (1976). Humanistic treatment of father daughter incest. In R.E. Helfer & C.H. Kempe (Eds.), *Child abuse and neglect: The family and the community* (pp. 143–158). Cambridge, MA: Ballinger.
Graves, P.A., & Sgroi, S.M. (1982). Law enforcement and child sexual abuse. In S.M. Sgroi (Ed.), *Handbook of clinical intervention in child sexual abuse* (pp. 309–332). Toronto: Lexington Books.
Howes, C. (1986, May 25). Incest: Dark secrets confronted. *Calgary Herald*, p. 1.
Pierce, R.L., & Pierce, L.H. (1985). Analysis of sexual abuse hotline reports. *Child Abuse and Neglect, 9*, 37–45.
Russell, A.B., & Trainor, C.M. (1984). *Trends in child abuse and neglect: A national perspective*. Denver, CO: American Humane Association.
Russell, D.E. (1983). The incidence and prevalence of intrafamilial and extrafamilial sexual abuse of female children. *Child Abuse and Neglect, 7*, 133–146.
Sgroi, S.M. (Ed.). (1982). *Handbook of clinical intervention in child sexual abuse*. Toronto: Lexington Books.
Shoalts, D. (1991, February 7). Action increasing on child abuse: Public awareness growing as more cases come to light. *The Globe and Mail*, p. 3.
Showers, J., Farber, E.D., Joseph, J.A., Oshins, L., & Johnson, C.F. (1983). Sexual victimization of boys: A three year study. *Health Values, 7*, 15–18.
Summit, R. (1980). *Typical characteristics of father-daughter incest: A guide for investigation*. Unpublished manuscript. Harbor UCLA Medical Center, Los Angeles, CA, 1–29.
Wilk, R.J., & McCarthy, C.R. (1986). Intervention in child sexual abuse: A survey of attitudes. *Social Casework, 67*, 20–26.

Journal of Child and Youth Care Special Issue Pages 65 – 76
 ISSN 0840–982X

Characteristics of Canadian Male and Female Child Sexual Abuse Victims

Barbara Thomlison
Faculty of Social Work, The University of Calgary
Michael Stephens
Alberta Family and Social Services, Calgary
J. William Cunes
Alberta Family and Social Services, Calgary
Richard M. Grinnell, Jr.
Faculty of Social Work, The University of Calgary
Judy Krysik
Faculty of Social Work, The University of Calgary

Abstract: This research presents timely Canadian-based data on child sexual abuse and compares variables that differentiate male and female victims. The information was compiled from the files of an Alberta Social Service region. Thirty substantiated cases of male child sexual abuse are compared with 161 substantiated cases of female child sexual abuse. Specific variables examined were: characteristics of the victim; the victim's family structure; a profile of the perpetrator; details pertaining to the sexually abusive occurrence, as well as outcome of the investigation.

Professional literature has documented the seriousness and effects of child sexual abuse (see, for example, Finkelhor, 1983). Research into this long-standing phenomenon has impacted knowledge development and service delivery in child protection and related fields (Pierce & Pierce, 1985a). Relevant organizations, innovative programs and an increased responsiveness to victims of sexual violence is a welcome development.

In spite of the proliferation of professional information, knowledge gaps pertaining to the differentiation of male and female victims of child sexual abuse continue to exist. Discriminating characteristics of sexually abused male and female children remain vague, implicating the quality of service delivery. Profiles of sexually abusive families and offenders lack detail and may result in children remaining at risk of further abuse.

An increase in the number of reported child sexual abuse cases raises many social work practice and research questions (Russell & Trainor, 1984). One of the greatest concerns of social workers today is that of the victim. The focus of this study was on the variables related to male and female victims in an attempt to present Canadian-based data about the victims of child sexual abuse.

METHODOLOGY

The Setting

In Canada, child welfare is a provincially-legislated responsibility. In Alberta, *The Province of Alberta Child Welfare Act* was passed by the Alberta Legislature on 31 May 1984, and proclaimed on 1 July 1985 (Alberta Social Services, 1984). This Act forms the basis for child welfare intervention in Alberta. The Government Ministry which administers the Child Welfare legislation for the Province of Alberta is Alberta Social Services. Any allegation of child sexual abuse must be referred to Alberta Social Services for investigation purposes.

The delivery of child welfare services in Alberta occurs through a decentralized system housed in six geographic regions. This study was carried out in one of Alberta's largest regions. The region includes a large metropolitan city and the surrounding rural territory. Five geographic offices offer an investigation/intake program within the region.

Operational Definition

To be consistent with the study's setting, we adopted the operational definition of child sexual abuse as legislated by the Province of Alberta Child Welfare Act: *A child is sexually abused if the child is inappropriately exposed or subjected to sexual contact, activity, or behavior,* Section 1(3) (c) p. 6 (Alberta Social Services, 1984).

Criteria for Sample Inclusion

Three criteria had to be satisfied in order for a child sexual abuse case to be included in the study. First, cases alleging child sexual abuse had to be referred to Alberta Social Services during the 1985 calendar year. The abuse itself did not have to occur in 1985, but must have been referred for investigation between 1 January 1985 and 31 December 1985.

The location to which the child sexual abuse was reported was the focus of the second criterion. To be included in this study the referral had to be made to the specified region mentioned above. The second criterion was met if the referral was actually investigated by a child welfare worker within the region under study.

The third criterion to be considered was assessment. The investigating social worker was required to have assessed that child sexual abuse had indeed occurred.

Sample

Having defined the sample using the above three criteria, the next step was to gather an inventory of all child welfare files. The study initially identified a preliminary group of 539 alleged victims who met the first two criteria. These 539 files were then reviewed to screen out those that did not meet the third criterion. This process rendered 191 cases in which the investigating social worker assessed that child sexual abuse had occurred. It is these 191 victims that form the final sample for this study.

Validity and Reliability

A data-gathering instrument was designed based upon a review of professional literature on child sexual abuse. Three employees of Alberta Social Services tested the instrument to affirm its content validity. Upon completion of this process, additions, modifications, and deletions in the format and operational definitions of the instrument were done to increase validity.

A test for interrater reliability rendered an error rate of less than one percent. Twenty percent of all files (109) included in this study were randomly checked for reliability of data collection. Seven errors were present in a total of 9,146 responses. Where there was error (disagreement between the principal data gatherer and the person checking reliability) the files were rechecked and corrections were made.

FINDINGS AND DISCUSSION

Five separate variables were highlighted in this article: victim, victim's family, perpetrator, occurrence, and outcome of the investigation. Each variable will be delineated into related sub-variables and data will be presented for both male and female victims.

Victim

Perhaps the largest body of literature concerning child sexual abuse is that which exists about the victim (Helfer, 1982). This study reports on five victim-related sub-variables: gender, age, relationship to the perpetrator, number of perpetrators, and previous history as a victim. These five sub-variables were chosen because of their prevalence in the literature.

The first of five sub-variables concerning the victim was the child's gender. Mrazek, Lynch, and Bentovim (1983) have reported that there are significantly larger numbers of reported female child sexual abuse victims than male victims. Other authors report similar findings (Erickson, Walbek, & Seely, 1988; Pierce & Pierce, 1985b). Generally, the literature indicates that between 80 percent to 90 percent of all reported victims are female (Pierce & Pierce, 1985b). Our analysis of Canadian data is in agreement with the findings presented above. As can be seen from Table 1, 84 percent of all reported victims of child sexual abuse were female.

Age of the victim at the onset of abuse was the second sub-variable which was examined. An interesting relationship between gender and age of the child sexual abuse victim is indicated by many studies. For example, the age of a male victim at the time of reporting was significantly lower than that for female victims (Russell, 1983). This study's findings were congruent with the literature where the mean age for males at the onset of abuse was eight years compared to 8.4 years for females.

Table 1
Victims of Child Sexual Abuse

VARIABLE	Male (*N* = 30) *n*	Female (*N* = 161) *n*
Mean Age of Child at Onset of Abuse		
Male 8.0 years	–	–
Female 8.4 years	–	–
Relationship to the Perpetrator		
Intrafamilial	15	131
Extrafamilial (Non-related)	15	23
Missing Data	0	7
Previous History as a Victim		
Yes	6	32
No	20	89
Missing Data	4	40
Number of Different Perpetrators		
Single Perpetrator	29	150
Multiple Perpetrators	1	10
Missing Data	0	1

The third sub-variable studied was the relationship of the victim to the perpetrator. Relationship to the perpetrator can be further broken down into two categories: intrafamilial or extrafamilial. For the purposes of this study, intrafamilial child sexual abuse occurred when there was a blood or legal familial relationship between the victim and the perpetrator. Extrafamilial child sexual abuse occurred when there was no blood or legal familial relationship between the victim and the perpetrator.

Pierce and Pierce (1985b), reported that a major difference between the male and female groups was that males were abused more frequently by persons other than father figures. Fifty percent of the males in this study were abused by non-related perpetrators. In comparison intrafamilial abuse among females occurred in 84 percent of the cases.

The child's previous history as a victim (i.e., physical abuse, neglect, sexual and emotional abuse), was the fourth sub-variable examined. Historical Canadian data (Corsini-Munt, 1982), reported that approximately one-third of all substantiated cases of child sexual abuse had been previously reported as allegations of abuse other than sexual. In this study, a previous history of child abuse recorded for 23 percent of the male victims and 26 percent of the female victims.

The final sub-variable examined was the number of different perpetrators involved with the victim. Evidence indicates that victims with multiple perpetrators have greater difficulty in treatment after the occurrences than do those with a single perpetrator (Greenburg, 1983). This study reports only slight variation in the number of different perpetrators among male and female victims. Ninety-seven percent of the male children were victimized by a single perpetrator, in comparison to 94 percent of the female children having a single perpetrator.

Victim's Family

Many variables have been associated with the family of the child sexual abuse victim. This section examines three: parental structure, other known family victims, and known prior sexual abuse of parents.

Table 2
Distribution of Victim's Family Subvariables

VARIABLE	Male (*N* = 30) *n*	Female (*N* = 161) *n*
Parental Structure		
Single Parent	20	51
Two Parent	10	105
Extended Family	0	2
Missing Data	0	3
Other Known Family Victims		
None	14	93
One	6	38
Two	10	16
Three	0	2
Missing Data	0	12
Known Prior Sexual Abuse of Parents		
Mother	5	24
Father	0	3
Both	0	1
None	17	0
Missing Data	8	133

Parental structure was the first of three sub-variables examined in respect to the victim's family. Family constellation is important to every child, especially in terms of risk to the child's safety and development. There is a large body of literature concerning family structure in relation to child sexual abuse (Dietz & Craft, 1980). This study defined parental structure as the adult(s) responsible for the child victim. Possibilities of family structure include: one natural parent, both natural parents, one natural parent and another parent, or an extended family living arrangement.

Upon reviewing the literature, Pierce and Pierce (1985b) found that the majority of male child sexual abuse victims resided with their natural mothers (92%), in comparison to 85 percent of female child sexual abuse victims. The major difference was that more male victims (38%) had no father figure in the home in comparison to female victims (12%) that had no father figure in the home. This study's findings are consistent in that 67 percent of the male subjects resided in single parent homes compared with 32 percent of the females.

Table 3
Distribution of Perpetrator Subvariables

VARIABLE	Male (*N* = 30) *n*	Female (*N* = 161) *n*
Mean Age of Perpetrator at Onset		
Male 22.5 years	–	–
Female 27.5 years	–	–
Perpetrator's Gender		
Male	28	158
Female	2	2
Missing Data	0	1
Previous History of Abuse as a Victim		
Yes	2	14
No	0	8
Missing Data	28	139
Previous History of Abuse as a Perpetrator		
Yes	17	74
No	0	0
Missing Data	13	87
Relationship to the Victim		
Father Role (Biological)	5	44
Father Role (Non-Biological)	3	46
Mother Role (Biological)	1	2
Female Sibling	0	2
Male Sibling	1	16
Uncle	1	11
Male Cousin	2	5
Grandfather	2	5
Significant Other (Non-Related)	15	23
Missing Data	0	7
Acknowledgement of Abuse		
Yes	5	43
No	9	39
Missing Data	16	79

The Perpetrator

There are many issues to be considered when examining the perpetrator in child sexual abuse. This section considers six sub-variables: the perpetrator's gender, mean age of the perpetrator at the onset of abusive behavior, previous history of abuse as a victim, previous history of abuse as a perpetrator, relationship to the victim and acknowledgment of the abuse.

The first sub-variable concerning the perpetrator was gender. There is an abundance of literature which indicates that males predominate in the commission of child sexual abuse (Finkelhor & Hotaling, 1984). This study's findings are clearly consistent with the literature in that 98 percent of the perpetrators were male.

The literature purports (see, for example, Pierce & Pierce, 1985a), that the mean age of the perpetrator was 34 years. This study's findings indicate that the mean age of the perpetrator (male and female combined) at the onset of abuse to be 27 years — seven years younger than the U.S. data.

Pierce and Pierce (1985b), found that males were significantly less likely to be abused by natural fathers than females when the perpetrator was the father figure. Another reported difference between male and female groups was that males were abused more frequently by persons other than the father figure. This study's findings were consistent with those reported by Pierce and Pierce. Twenty-nine percent of females were sexually abused by the natural father in comparison to 17 percent of male victims. Fifty percent of the male victims were sexually abused by a non-related perpetrator, in comparison to 15 percent of the female victims. Abuse was acknowledged more frequently when the victim was female (52%) than when the victim was male (36%).

The Occurrence

The fourth variable that plays an important role in the study of child sexual abuse is the occurrence itself. Three sub-variables related to the occurrence were considered: the primary sexual act, duration of the abuse, and the frequency of occurrence.

The first sub-variable regarding the occurrence is the primary sexual act. Attitudes toward child sexual abuse are documented to be influenced by the abusive activities that occur (Wilk & McCarthy, 1986). There are both legal and practical distinctions between vaginal or anal penetration and incidents such as exposure or fondling, especially with regard to the degree of injury. Also related to the type of activity is the question of upon whom the sexual act was performed. The victim may be coerced into performing a sexual act on the perpetrator just as frequently as the perpetrator victimizes the child.

Table 4
Distribution of Occurrence Subvariables

VARIABLE	Male (*N* = 30) *n*	Female (*N* = 161) *n*
Mean Duration of Abuse (in months)		
Male 15.0	–	–
Female 21.7	–	–
Primary Sexual Act		
Exposure	3	6
Fondling of Genitalia	13	66
Cunnilingus	1	2
Fellatio	4	1
Vaginal Penetration	0	40
Attempted Vaginal Penetration	0	12
Dry Intercourse	1	3
Anal Penetration	3	5
Kissing	0	2
Not Classified	2	6
Missing Data	3	18
Frequency		
Single Occurrence	4	30
Multiple Occurrence	20	106
Missing Data	6	25

Rimza and Niggeman (1982) reported vaginal contact in 46 percent of female child sexual abuse cases and anal or oral contact in 17 percent of the cases. In comparison, anal contact was reported by 58 percent of the male victims. This study found vaginal contact occurred in 32 percent of the offences against the female child. Three percent of the occurrences involved anal penetration, and one percent involved fellatio. In contrast, males experienced anal penetration in 11 percent of the occurrences, and fellatio in 15 percent.

The second sub-variable to be considered in regard to occurrence is the duration of abuse. Studies indicate large numbers of child sexual abuse situations continue for years prior to the victim's disclosure to a person in authority (Russell & Trainor, 1984). Again this study was congruent with the literature. The mean duration of abuse for male victims was 15 months compared to 21.7 months for female victims. There are difficulties, however, in regard to interpreting child sexual abuse data pertaining to males. The literature suggests that persons having knowledge of child sexual abuse involving a male victim, including the victim himself, are less likely to report the abuse for fear the disclosure will label the child as a homosexual (Pierce & Pierce, 1985b).

This creates difficulty in determining the incidence and prevalence of sexual abuse involving the male child.

Frequency of occurrence in child sexual abuse has been given due attention in the literature (Finkelhor, 1983). The difference between a single occurrence and multiple occurrences is an important consideration in victim treatment and perpetrator disposition. Berliner and Conte (1981) have reported that the majority of cases (66%) include multiple occurrences. This study found the data for male and female victims to be similar in regard to this variable. Eighty-three percent of the cases involving the male child were multiple incidents compared to 78 percent of the cases involving the female child.

Disposition and Outcome

The magnitude of child sexual abuse cases brings into question the effectiveness and consistency of action by the police, the criminal justice system and child protection workers. This section examines four sub-variables related to investigation and outcome in cases of child sexual abuse: the pursuance of criminal charges, removal of the child from the home, removal of the perpetrator from the home in instances of intrafamilial abuse, and child welfare status of the case following investigation.

Table 5
Distribution of Disposition and Outcome Subvariables

VARIABLE	Male (*N* = 30) *n*	Female (*N* = 161) *n*
Charges Laid		
Yes	7	48
No	14	78
Missing Data	9	35
Child Removed from Home		
Yes	6	38
No	23	117
Missing Data	1	6
Perpetrator Removed		
Yes	12	76
No	8	52
Missing Data	7	3
Case Status After Investigation		
Opened	13	97
Closed	17	63
Missing Data	0	1

Criminal action against the alleged offender is the most controversial aspect of the problem of child sexual abuse. In opposition, criminal action is considered detrimental to the needs of the child, the family, and the rehabilitation of the offender. In support, criminal action is considered necessary for treatment, the fulfillment of justice and for the deterrence of further abuse (Finkelhor, 1983). In this study charges were more often not placed than placed for both male and female victims.

Finkelhor (1983) reported that, on the whole, children received placements at home or outside of the home in accordance with their desires. A preference to be placed outside the home was more likely to be met than a preference to stay. Removing the child from the home is one recourse that is readily available to child protection workers in Alberta. This study found that the male victim was removed from the home in 211 percent of the cases, compared to 25 percent for the female victims.

The fourth sub-variable, child welfare status following investigation, was the only sub-variable reporting any major difference between the male and female victim groups. Sixty-one percent of the cases involving a female victim remained open, in comparison to 43 percent of the cases involving a male child. Erickson, Walbek and Seely (1988), reported that the recidivism history among child sexual abuse offenders to be somewhat higher (35%) than usual for felony convictions (20%). The literature supports that timing and opportunity for repeated contact influences behavior (Finkelhor, 1983). Intrafamilial cases ordinarily involve multiple contact over time, with gradual progression from fondling to attempted penetration. Therefore, we would expect status after investigation to be more dependent on intra or extrafamilial abuse than on the gender of the victim.

IMPLICATIONS AND SUMMARY

Monitoring the profiles of the victim, the family, and the perpetrator have great implications for human service professionals concerned with child sexual abuse. Community education can be focused to the population with the greatest need. Armed with characteristic data child protection workers may be able to identify the victim, therefore preventing further abuse.

In constructing the five tables presented in this study, the authors found a great deal of missing data. Missing information for any one variable ranged as high as 87 percent. This has implications for the development of a standardized data collection format to be used in child sexual abuse investigations.

The similarity of Canadian data to that from the United States have implications for further service development. The United States has a proliferation of information concerning child sexual abuse. Treatment programs, policy makers and child care workers could benefit from the knowledge developed in the US. Further study is necessary, however, to validate the apparent similarities.

In summary, this research note has presented timely Canadian-based data on male and female victims of child sexual abuse. The information was compiled from the files of one Alberta Social Service region. Specific variables described were: characteristics of the victim; the victim's family structure; a profile of the perpetrator; the sexually abusive occurrence; as well as investigation and outcome variables.

The findings of this study indicate that the male and female sexual abuse victim can be differentiated on a number of variables. Therefore, it is essential that policy makers, criminal justice personnel and child protection workers be aware of the characteristic differences and develop treatment programs accordingly. We cannot assume that programs developed to serve the norm (i.e., the female child), will be effective with the male child and his family. Furthermore, this type of analysis is necessary to determine if the quality of service thus far has been adequate or indiscriminate and inconsistent.

REFERENCES

Alberta Social Services. (1984). *Province of Alberta child welfare act.* Edmonton, AB: Queen's Printer.

Berliner, L., & Conte, J.R. (1981). Sexual abuse of children: Implications for practice. *Social Casework, 62*, 601–606.

Corsini-Munt, L.A. (1982). A Canadian study: Sexual abuse of children and adolescents. In B. Schlesinger (Ed.), *Sexual abuse of children: A resource guide and annotated bibliography* (pp. 116–133). Toronto: University of Toronto Press.

Dietz, C.A., & Craft, J.L. (1980). Family dynamics of incest: A new perspective. *Social Casework, 61*, 602–609.

Erickson, W.D., Walbek, N.H., & Seely, R.K. (1988). Behavior patterns of child molesters. *Archives of Sexual Behavior, 7*(1), 77–86.

Finkelhor, D. (1983). Removing the child — prosecuting the offender in cases of sexual abuse: Evidence from the national reporting system for child abuse and neglect. *Child Abuse and Neglect, 7*, 195–205.

Finkelhor, D., & Hotaling, G.T. (1984). Sexual abuse in the national incidence study of child abuse and neglect. *Child Abuse and Neglect, 8*, 23–33.

Greenburg, N. (1983). Remarks to the national medical center's conference on sexual abuse. In D. Finkelhor. *Child abuse and neglect, 7*, 195–205.

Helfer, R.E. (1982). A review of the literature on the prevention of child abuse and neglect. *Child Abuse and Neglect, 6*, 251–266.

Mrazek, P.J., Lynch, M.A., & Bentovim, A. (1983). Sexual abuse of children in the United Kingdom. *Child Abuse and Neglect, 7*, 147–153.

Pierce, R.L., & Pierce, L.H. (1985a). Analysis of sexual abuse hotline reports. *Child Abuse and Neglect, 9*, 37–45.

Pierce, R.L., & Pierce, L.H. (1985b). The sexually abused child: A comparison of male and female victims. *Child Abuse and Neglect, 9*, 191–199.

Rimza, M., & Niggeman, E. (1982). Medical evaluation of sexually abused children: A review of 311 cases. *Pediatrics, 69*, 8–14.

Russell, D.E. (1983). The incidence and prevalence of intrafamilial and extrafamilial sexual abuse of female children. *Child Abuse and Neglect, 7*, 133–146.

Russell, A.B., & Trainor, C.M. (1984). *Trends in child abuse and neglect: A national perspective*. Denver, CO: American Human Association.

Wilk, R.J., & McCarthy, C.R. (1986). Intervention in child sexual abuse: A survey of attitudes. *Social Casework, 67*, 20–26.

Journal of Child and Youth Care Special Issue Pages 77 – 85
 ISSN 0840–982X

A Model for Immediate Voluntary Assessment of Male Adolescent Sex Offenders

David Baird
Children's Aid Society of Metropolitan Toronto

Abstract: This paper contends that some male adolescent sexual offenders who have been charged and have admitted their guilt can benefit from a pre-court sexual-offence-specific voluntary assessment. These offenders can be monitored for risk of re-offending as well as assessed for amenability for future treatment. Further, a detailed history of sexual offences and/or victimizations as well as social and familial factors can be ascertained. Active participation in an assessment process can be a means of monitoring an offender and holding him immediately accountable and responsible for his abusive behaviour. The adolescent also has his defence mechanisms of minimization and rationalization confronted before they become further ingrained. The assessment requires the informed consent of the adolescent sexual offender and their parent(s) or guardian(s). Legal counsel is strongly recommended for the family before agreement on becoming involved in the assessment program. This model utilizes a combination of assessment and treatment components in order to collect information, monitor risk and develop amenability for treatment. Therefore, treatment objectives such as offender accountability and responsibility become an integral part of a process that remains primarily an assessment.

ASSESSMENT LIMITATIONS

In the Metro Toronto area, a cooperative team of police officers and Children's Aid Society social workers systematically investigate allegations of child sexual abuse. Periodically, these investigations determine the existence of an adolescent sexual offender.

Few adolescents will admit to sexually abusing a younger child. Of those that do, there are but a fewer number who will voluntarily agree to a detailed assessment. Of this group there are some who will be discouraged from participation by parent(s) and/lawyers.

The adolescent who denies that he has committed the alleged offence has the right to maintain his innocence through to the court date and cannot be considered for this model. This teenager may be appropriate for assessment of non-sexual-offence-specific problems such as family, environment or other special conflicts. The methodology of this model is not appropriate for the denying adolescent.

The adolescent with a major mental disorder or neurological problem will be more appropriately assessed through psychiatric or other specialized means. It is the adolescent who has admitted to the sexual offending, does not have a major mental health problem and has given informed consent to his participation in this assessment who can be given the opportunity to benefit from immediate intervention.

IMMEDIATE ASSESSMENT RATIONALE

There is generally a time frame of several months between an adolescent being charged and then entering a plea in court. If the adolescent has admitted to the sexual offence for which he had been charged, then he should be afforded the opportunity to become involved in an assessment process right away. There are several risks involved in not affording him this opportunity. One such risk is that the adolescent who is not involved in an assessment process will have his behaviour monitored mainly by himself and possibly by his parents. Such self or family monitoring should be considered an inappropriate risk for society in that most families of adolescent sexual offenders have inherent degrees of minimization, rationalization and denial of the adolescent's behaviour. Examples of this are that some offenders have depersonalized the abuse to the extent that they have convinced themselves that no one was harmed or victimized. Others feel that their behaviour was not wrong because the victim did not say no. There are a multitude of such minimizations and rationalizations that operate within the mind of the adolescent sexual offender.

Often parents of offenders want desperately to believe in any minimization or rationalization that will "explain" their adolescent behaviour. At times this desperation includes grasping onto denial of the abuse. Parents that buy into such "explanations" decrease their ability to monitor their teen's behaviour. Given time this pattern of minimization, rationalization and denial can strengthen into an attitude that totally undermines the seriousness of what the adolescent had done, and even undermines the charges that were levied. The adolescent offender who is involved in an immediate assessment has his minimizations and rationalizations confronted before they become further ingrained.

Many of these defense mechanisms can be challenged using facts about differences between offender and victim in areas of age, size and level of power, authority, relationship and trust. By replacing the minimizations and rationalizations with the facts of the sexually abusive offence, the adolescent can begin the process of assuming accountability and responsibility for his behaviour. This is the process of having the adolescent offender assume total responsibility for the abuse and which is a primary goal of treatment rather than assessment. Establishing the premise and need to do so is a rationale, however.

ASSESSMENT GOALS

The sexual offence specific assessment has five goals:

1. Monitor the risk of re-offending.
2. Develop the offender's amenability for treatment.
3. Compile a personal history of sexual, social and family dynamics.
4. Compile a treatment needs evaluation.
5. Prepare an assessment report for court.

Assumption Goals

It is assumed that the investigative team has determined the appropriateness of intervention in that a crime has been committed, charges have been laid and proper guidelines have been followed to ensure that the behaviour is not:

a) normal sexual activity;
b) inappropriate solitary sexual activity of a non-aggressive manner (Groth & Laredo, 1981).

It is assumed that the investigative team has made an initial determination that the adolescent offender being referred presents a low enough risk of re-offending that he can remain in his own community, pending assessment recommendations and for court decisions.

High risk factors that indicate the inappropriateness of community treatment are:

1. repeated offence for which an offender has already received treatment;
2. the offence involved violence, physical force, use or threat of use of a weapon;
3. evidence of progressive increase in the force used to commit a repeated offence;
4. the offence was predatory, ritualistic, continued despite the victim's expression of distress; and
5. the offender's significant intellectual deficits limit their [sic] ability to learn from the consequences of their [sic] behaviour (Knopp, 1985).

A further assumption is that the investigative team has evidenced some indicators in the offender of amenability to an assessment program.

Goal #1: Monitor the Risk of Re-offending

A voluntary adolescent sexual offender assessment can either validate or repudiate the initial investigative determination of risk for re-offending.

The level of risk can be revised at any time that new information materializes as part of the ongoing assessment. At any time that the assessment program details moderate or high risk of re-offending, case conferencing with the investigating team needs to occur to determine continued suitability of community placement of offender. At the minimum, the risk of re-offending should be calculated at the beginning and end of the assessment.[1]

A useful tool for assessing risk is the Wenet and Clark (1983) 37 point checklist of clinical risk criteria, which they have divided into low, moderate, or high risk of re-offending.

Goal #2: Develop the Amenability for Treatment

The initial willingness of the adolescent offender to be involved demonstrates a basic amenability to the assessment process.

The therapeutic task is to foster this basic amenability during the assessment process and develop an amenability to a treatment programme. An effective means of developing this amenability is through the use of an authoritative yet empathetic counselling style. The adolescent offender who feels understood and supported during the difficult task of explaining his abusive behaviour will usually be more amenable to the processes of assessment and subsequent treatment.

This authoritative and empathetic style can influence the offender to be accountable for his behaviour while also feeling that all of the factors impacting on such behaviours are understood.

Steen and Monnette (1989) list offender characteristics that can influence amenability as well as risk. They list the offender's age and sophistication, honesty, responsibility, empathy, motivation, adjustment, compulsivity, substance abuse, intellectual capacity, victimization and previous treatment history or previous abuse. The authors combine these characteristics with offence and situation characteristics to produce a detailed categorizing of either:

a) high amenability and low risk;
b) medium amenability and medium risk;
c) low amenability and high risk (Steen & Monnette, 1989).

Goal #3: Compile a Personal History of Sexual, Social and Family Dynamics

A complete assessment requires personal history data from the offender, his family and other appropriate sources.

The sexual history should address offending behaviours, sexual victimization history and sexual attitudes. Social factors include the influence of peers, pornography and substance abuse. Family dynamics that impact include relationship patterns and roles, uses of power, authority and any other form of abuse.

This model utilizes oral questioning to elicit the personal history data. Other authors such as Steen and Monnette (1989), make excellent use of written questionnaires of the adolescent and his parents. A combination of oral and written questionnaires could be most beneficial to elicit this information.

Goal #4: Compile a Treatment-needs Evaluation

A treatment-needs evaluation considers short and long-term objectives for the adolescent offender and his family. Treatment does not necessarily have to be long term, nor does it have to involve individual and group therapy. Recommendations may sometimes be made as part of the assessment, regarding the most appropriate length and mode of therapy in each adolescent offender case. Most recommendations for treatment involve expectations of both group and individual counselling. From the very first contact with the offender, work needs to be done to "sell" the idea of the need for treatment following assessment. At various stages where the offender is making good progress, treatment themes can be introduced that begin to demonstrate to the offender that there are many ways in which professional intervention can help him resolve many different problem areas.

It is also necessary to engage the parent(s) or guardian(s) from the onset of assessment. It is crucial that the parents understand that they have a role not only to provide assessment information, such as family background, but they also can best help the adolescent through regular, active participation in assessment and later, treatment. Bi-weekly parent sessions with the offender can service several functions. Information given by the offender can be checked and parents can be informed of issues with which they can assist their adolescent. The parents can begin to understand some of the dynamics of their teen's abuse and how other factors interplay in his abusive behaviour. The offender can see his parents actively involved in supporting, trying to understand and assist him and each other through this difficult process.

Parents need to be made aware that offending behaviour does not necessarily stop during the assessment period. As a result, parents have to provide a monitoring force for their adolescent. Rules that prohibit access to younger children, such as "no babysitting" need to be enforced. A minimum parental contact schedule would be monthly sessions. Parental contact that is less than monthly is not nearly as helpful to the above goals and it definitely limits the scope of the assessment.

Goal #5: Prepare an Assessment Report for Court

The time frame for this assessment involves the date of referral to the date of court. Usually this is 10 to 15 weeks but it can be even longer. Within this period of time the offender and his family need to initially decide on whether to become involved and they need time at the end of the assessment to digest the assessment reports, information and recommendations. If the time frame is short to begin with, the assessment and the report may not be fully completed in time to adequately compile all necessary information. The assessment report can be submitted with the necessary limitations noted. (See methodology for discussion on the time of the release of the assessment report to the court.)

The headings currently in use for this model are as follows:

1. DURATION:
   - length of assessment.
2. FORMAT:
   - who was seen and how often.
   - include contacts with victim(s) and other resources.
3. ASSESSMENT MATERIAL:

i. Details of sexually abusive behaviour:
   - offenders' behaviour and own sexual victimization.
   - any progressions in frequency or severity.

ii. Details of victimization strategies:
   - how the victim was engaged in the abuse.
   - what inducements were used.
   - what threats, coercion or force was employed.
   - how secrecy was established and maintained.

iii. Offender's attitudes towards:
   - his offence(s) -
   - the degree of honesty, congruence, empathy, remorse, guilt, shame, responsibility.
   - his victim(s) -
   - include attitude towards females and males in general and those he offended specifically.
   - the assessment process -
   - amenability.

iv. Interpersonal functioning — how the offender interrelates with:
   - family.
   - friends.
   - peers.
   - significant others.
   - offender's ability to form and maintain relationships.
   - social skills.

v. Psychological functioning:
   - sexual offence specific psychological testing.[2]

vi. Family Issues:
   - relationships between family members.
   - dysfunctional behaviour.
   - reactions to disclosure of sexual abuse.

- historical patterns of any form of abuse.
- traumatic family events.
- parental responses, attitudes and amenability to assessment process.

vii. Recommendations:

- any need for further assessment.
- degree of amenability for treatment.
- treatment referral options.
- implications of risk assessment.

INFORMED CONSENT

The adolescent and his parents must completely understand the nature and legality of the assessment process before it begins. It is not enough that passive consent be given.

Discussion of the pros and cons of involvement in the assessment which includes the possible consequences, must occur and be understood in order that an informed consent is obtained. The family needs to know that participation in the assessment may evoke additional disclosures of sexual offences that will be reported to the police and potentially can result in further charges.

The family also needs to understand that the assessment report will outline the degrees of honesty, congruence, responsibility, empathy, and other feelings that the adolescent demonstrates. Should the report favourably address the adolescent's honesty and congruence with other known case facts, then it can be in the offender's best interest for the court to recognize this. It also can be in the adolescent's best interest to have a report that states that he is a good candidate for a treatment programme as demonstrated partly through participation and cooperation during assessment. Any examples with which the court can be presented that speak to accepting responsibility, developing victim empathy or behavioural changes can be beneficial for the adolescent offender.

Discussions also need to occur with the family regarding confidentiality, information releases and the assessment report before consent is given. The less confidentiality that exists and the more information that is available, the more complete the assessment will be. There also has to be communication between the helping professions involved with the family. Information releases need to be obtained between agencies working with the families of offender(s) and victim(s) to correlate the details of the abuse(s). The concept of correlating evidence is one that members of the family should discuss with their lawyer in consideration of the legal implications.

The adolescent offender and his parents should be informed that the assessment report will be issued to the court immediately following his plea of guilt. The timing of the release of the report to the court is important for two reasons.

A thorough assessment report that includes recommendations for future therapy can be of great assistance to the court for sentencing purposes. At the court's discretion, the report can be substituted for other assessment procedures and in this way, an offender can be sentenced quickly following his plea of guilt without the delay imposed by the need for a court clinic assessment. The assessment report cannot be released before a finding of guilt which precludes the report being submitted before a plea of guilt or innocence.

When presenting the rationale for becoming involved in the assessment program, it should be explained that the program reserves the right to end the assessment should several conditions warrant this action. These conditions include an offender missing a substantial number of sessions, an offender repeatedly changing versions of what happened, or an offender displaying indications that the program no longer seems voluntary for him. Should the offender find that he is close to detailing activities, fantasies, thoughts or feelings that he does not feel comfortable having documented, then the offender, with assistance, needs to have the freedom to decide voluntarily whether to remain involved. Hopefully the offender has considered the implications of this before beginning the assessment, but should this materialize within the assessment itself, the program needs to carefully allow for voluntary decision making by the offender. This does not preclude the assessment report detailing the dilemma in which the offender has found himself.

CONCLUSION

It can take weeks or months for the offender to come to the realization that sexual offending is a problem that needs therapeutic intervention to resolve. The adolescent offender who is involved in an immediate assessment program can begin to look at his problem right away. He can think about his interpersonal functioning; he can begin to see how family dynamics influence his behaviour. The adolescent offender can be encouraged to see sexually abusive behaviour as a problem that is going to take time and treatment to work out.

At his initial assessment meeting, Tony confidently asserted that he was sure he would not re-offend sexually. When asked why he felt so sure, Tony replied that after he abused his younger brother he promised himself that it would not happen again. Tony was then asked to explain why the abuse had happened several times already and he looked extremely surprised and said, "That's your job to find out why!" Tony, like many adolescent offenders, pretended to appear confidently in control of his sexually abusive behaviour. It was weeks later that he admitted to feeling very fearful of re-offending.

During the time frame of the assessment the adolescent offender can be held accountable, responsible, and to a degree, can be monitored, for his sexually abusive behaviour. With a completed written assessment and finding of guilt, the adolescent offender can emerge from the court proceedings with an amenable attitude for treatment already in place, rather than being ordered into court clinic assessment. There also is a chance that, like Tony, the adolescent offender has in mind some answers as to why the abuse occurred and reoccurred and perhaps will learn how to reduce the risk of the abuse occurring again.

NOTES

1. The Preliminary Report from the National Task Force on Juvenile Sexual Offending (1988) lists 34 factors that can influence the assessment of risk of re-offending.
2. The adolescent Perpetrator Network Uniform Data Collection System lists 16 psychological tests that may be useful for adolescent offenders (Ryan, 1986).

REFERENCES

Groth, A.N., & Loredo, C.M. (1981). Juvenile sex offenders: Guidelines for assessment. *International Journal of Offender Therapy and Comparative Criminology, 25*(1), 32–33.

Knopp, F.H. (1985). *The youthful sex offender: The rationale and goals of early intervention and treatment.* Syracuse, NY: Safer Society Press.

National Adolescent Perpetrator Network. (1988). Preliminary report from the National Task Force on Juvenile Sexual Offending, 1988. *Juvenile and Family Court Journal, 39*(2), 21.

Ryan, G. (1986). Initial Evaluation/Assessment Form. Adolescent perpetrator network uniform data collection system. Adolescent Perpetrator Network, National Centre, 1205 Oneida St., Denver, CO, 80262–2944.

Steen, C., & Monnette, B. (1989). *Treating adolescent sex offenders in the community.* Springfield, IL: Charles C. Thomas.

Wenet, G.A., & Clark, T.R. (1983). *Decision criterion.* Juvenile Sexual Offender Programme. Seattle, WA: University of Washington.

Journal of Child and Youth Care Special Issue Pages 87 – 101
 ISSN 0840–982X

Male Adolescent Sex Offenders: A Comparison of Two Treatment Approaches

Billie Y. Orr
Department of Educational Psychology
The University of Calgary

Abstract: The fact that some male adolescent sex offenders have been the victim of sexual abuse raises important etiological questions regarding thorough understanding and effective treatment of this multifaceted, complex human problem. The present paper addresses treatment issues and goals from a psychodynamic and social learning perspective. Concepts, hypotheses and methods of intervention common to each theory are reviewed. It is concluded that a combination of these two approaches is the most efficacious intervention.

A burgeoning interest in the general area of sexual abuse can be discerned in a broad spectrum of applied and research communities. Finkelhor's (1984) explanation of this reality credits the concerns voiced by the women's movement (Herman, 1984) and child protection services (Kemp & Williams, 1982). Collectively, these two groups have been responsible for consciousness raising and have provided the impetus for political, societal, community, and agency responsiveness and change.

Of the numerous significant and ripple effects emanating from mass cognizance of this social issue, we have witnessed substantial increases in disclosure of sexual abuse (Waterman & Lusk, 1986), a developing concern regarding false allegations (Emans, 1988; Mantell, 1988; Yates & Musty, 1988), and greater attention paid to the understanding, assessment and treatment of the adolescent offender (Ageton, 1983; Davis & Leitenberg, 1987; Fehrenbach & Monastersky, 1988; Saunders & Awad, 1988).

Research findings based on retrospective techniques have identified childhood sexual abuse in the histories of many adult sex offenders (Groth, 1979; Seghorn, Prentky, & Boucher, 1987). Similar findings with samples of adolescent perpetrators have now been well documented (Becker, Kaplan, Cunningham-Rathner, & Kavoussi, 1986; Burgess, Hartman, & McCormack, 1987; Davis & Leitenberg, 1987; Finkelhor & Browne, 1985; Freeman-Longo, 1986; Rowe, 1988; Ryan, Lane, Davis, & Isaac, 1987; Saunders & Awad, 1988) and raise pertinent etiological questions related to accurate conceptualizations and effective treatment of this complex human problem.

The present paper will address the significance of this finding for the treatment of the male adolescent sex offender from two contrasted theoretical models: psychodynamic and social learning. Important treatment issues and goals associated with this clinical population that transcend particular theories and therapeutic methods of change will be identified. An outline of psychodynamic and social learning concepts and hypotheses related to this young offender's present crime and past victimization will be presented in conjunction with intervention strategies commonly employed by proponents of each model. Conclusions will examine each model's efficacy with respect to issues and goals as stated.

TREATMENT ISSUES

Risk of Reoffending

Although the question, "What is the likelihood that this particular sex offender will commit another sexual offence?" is one that is addressed during the assessment phase, it is a question that must be continually re-evaluated throughout the treatment process. Treatment decisions, grounded in sound clinical judgment, are guided by the psychologist's professional code of ethics (American Psychological Association, 1981; Canadian Psychological Association, 1986a, 1986b) that mandate concern for the welfare of the client and responsibility to society. Owing in part to the multifaceted, complex nature of sexual abuse, a lack of consistency in the literature regarding the precise definition of sexually abusive behaviour, and a paucity of controlled experimental studies (Davis & Leitenberg, 1987), a well-defined set of predictor variables does not presently exist.

Based on current knowledge, the prediction of risk, according to Groth (1978), can be assessed by addressing the following questions: (a) To what extent does the offence derive from internal, psychological determinants, and to what degree does the behaviour result from external factors?; and (b) what are the environmental conditions that increase the probability of offending, and what are the chances these conditions will exist? In terms of treatment and methods of intervention, the therapist will bear in mind the young person's strengths and weaknesses related to specific risk factors associated with his life.

Dangerousness

Although dangerousness is connected to the risk of re-offending issue, the concerns explored in assessing the potential danger the adolescent constitutes to a victim are relatively well defined and shed light on the significance of the individual's own victimization. Groth (1978) outlined four factors that contribute to the severity of psychological and/or emotional trauma to the victim and thus determine dangerousness: (a) the nature of the relationship between offender and victim; (b) duration of sexual contact; (c) type of sexual activity occurring in the abuse situations; and (d) the degree of force or aggression directed toward the victim.

Treatment Goals

Although the ultimate goal of any treatment program is the discontinuance of sexually inappropriate behaviour (Greer & Stuart, 1983), progressive steps toward this end that are generally agreed upon include: (a) the offender needs to acknowledge that he did in fact commit the offence without projecting blame; (b) the young person is held responsible and accountable for his actions and some form of restitution is made; (c) the adolescent needs to be aware of the chain of events and patterns of behaviour and/or emotion that lead up to sexual acting-out; and (d) the offender must be able to develop alternative, acceptable ways of expressing his emotion, gratifying his needs, and/or controlling his impulsive behaviours (Groth, 1978; Kahn & Lafond, 1988; Rowe, 1988; Ryan, Lane, Davis, & Isaac, 1987; Smets & Cebula, 1987). To the extent that psychodynamic or social learning models achieve these goals then treatment has been beneficial.

PSYCHODYNAMIC MODELS

Concepts and Hypotheses

Lerner's (1987) review of current psychodynamic models of thinking about adolescence noted that contemporary psychoanalytic theory is increasingly becoming a developmental psychology of the self and object relations. From this viewpoint human behaviour is understood in terms of various developmental, environmental, and intrapsychic factors, motivated by the gratification of idiosyncratic needs and the defence against anxiety. An individual's actions, however maladaptive, can be understood by identifying childhood experiences, the meaning ascribed to those experiences, and the nature of significant interpersonal relationships that impacted on and served to shape personality development and current psychological adjustment. Adolescent behaviour then is not random rebellious expressions of unconscious drives and libidinal energies influenced predominantly by the demands of the peer culture. For the most part, it is a meaningful though not necessarily conscious attempt to assert autonomy, achieve individuation from the family of origin, regulate internal tensions, cope with conflicts and integrate one's experiences into a stable and coherent personal identity. To the extent that one's experiences have been positive, self-affirming and growth-producing, and to the extent that one's interpersonal relationships with parents and peers have been characterized by support, understanding, mutual trust and emotional responsiveness, a healthy self-concept and adaptive skills of socialization and psychological functioning will likely result.

For the adolescent male who has been subjected to sexual abuse in childhood, and whose biological and psychoneurological development has been unremarkable (Lewis, Shanok, & Pincus, 1981), the requirements for adaptive adjustment will not have been met. His inappropriate and possibly dangerous sexual behaviour might be constructively regarded as symptomatic of pathological early experiences, unmet needs and unresolved internal conflicts.

The relationship between the young offender and his perpetrator becomes a significant variable in terms of understanding the impact of his victimization. It is generally agreed that the closer the emotional relationship, the greater the risk of the victim experiencing psychological trauma (Groth, 1978). If the abuser was a parent or adult guardian with whom the child had developed a sense of trust and to whom he looked for nurturance and protection, the effect of the abuse would be more serious that if the offender was a stranger. Also, if the abuser was a male, the impact would be more serious yet, as it would have a major impact on the adolescent's developing sexual identity (Breer, 1987; Finkelhor & Browne, 1985; Nasjleti, 1986).

Given that psychodynamic theory states that "normative development demands that the adolescent boy identify with his father or father figure" (Lerner, 1987 cited Blos, 1979, p. 66), it becomes clear that the most traumatic experience would probably be in the experience of father-son sexual abuse. The father is essentially represented in idealized form in the developing male child's ego ideal. Through strong identification with the abusing father and the internalization of the father's morals and values, the child comes to see himself in his adolescence as like his father. Given that the ego ideal strives for perfection, in this case emulation of father, and given that the striving for perfection produces a sense of well-being and narcissistic self-idealization, the young offender might take pride in his sexually aggressive or exploitive behaviours. His lack of individual goals, values and clear sexual identity produce a feeling of insecurity and instability that he may effectively overcome by putting an increasing premium on sexual prowess for self-assertion and self-esteem.

The duration of sexual contact and the child's age will both be important variables in understanding the traumatizing effect of the adolescent's past victimization. Repeated contacts over a long period of time is more damaging to the developing child's ego and concept of self than a single incident. Continuous violation of the child's body creates an overall feeling of powerlessness and helplessness such that the child comes to believe that he has virtually no control over what happens to him. Anger and resentment combine with guilt and fear creating emotional confusion, conflict and instability. With a developing awareness of sexual impulses in adolescence and deep-seated insecurities regarding his sexual orientation, the sexually abusive behaviour if directed toward females, serves to assure the young offender that he is capable of heterosexual arousal. His need to enhance an overall low level of self-esteem and to feel valuable and sexually attractive to the other gender, might be expressed in convictions that his victims were aroused by his behaviour. If the adolescent is choosing young male victims this would represent his emotional immaturity and psychological regression as he attempts to satisfy his unmet needs of boyhood through his adolescent needs for sexual outlets.

The type of sexual activity that occurred historically in the young offender's role of victim will probably be played out in his new role as offender. Finkelhor (1984) noted that bizarre sexual acts teach the child to make long lasting associations between objects or body parts and experiences of physical pleasure. The adolescent may fetishize parts of the anatomy and reinforce these associations in his masturbatory fantasies which he then acts out in sexually abusive behaviours. Groth (1978) pointed out that the sexual acts the child was subjected to are more traumatic if they involved physical contact as opposed to exhibitionism or voyeurism, and that the negative impact increases with invasion of the child's body with sexual penetration being more harmful than noncoital sexual activity. The more the child is invaded the more he is made to feel helpless and the stronger his consequent feelings of rage and fear. When these emotions are combined with the physical pleasure of sexual arousal, the young offender's acting-out behaviours are more apt to be aggressive and the danger he presents to the community is increased.

Groth and his colleagues (Groth & Hobson, 1983; Groth, Hobson, & Gary, 1982) have drawn a distinction between the offender who uses physical force and aggression and the one who bribes or seduces his victims into sexual contacts. It seems that the central difference between the two subgroups of sex offenders is one of power and control. The notion of power as a motivating variable has been given considerable attention (Finkelhor &Browne, 1985; Groth & Hobson, 1983; Handy & Cammaert, 1985; Herman, 1984).

The specifics of the adolescent's current abusive behaviour and his past victimization will shed light on the relevance of the power construct in terms of the meaning he has attributed to his role as victim and the manner in which he attempts to assert control over events in his life now. It may be that his abusive actions represent a re-enactment of the sexual offences he was subjected to and serve as a maladaptive attempt to resolve early trauma and gain a sense of personal power and control that he did not have in his role as victim (Groth, 1979). An alternative or possibly co-existing dynamic is that of identification with the offender such that the repetition of sexually assaultive acts are perceived to be normative expressions of sexual impulses. Denial of responsibility, denial of the victim's experience, projection of blame, and lack of empathy are the defences used to absolve himself of guilt and anxiety.

Intervention

In general, psychodynamic psychotherapy seeks to expand awareness of and conscious control over intrapsychic, interpersonal and/or environmental events that are creating psychological difficulties (Weiner, 1976). Based on a trusting therapeutic relationship and a non-threatening, safe environment, exploratory and interpretive procedures are utilized to meet this end. Weiner also pointed out that requirements for participation in and maximum benefit from this introspective treatment method include: (a) a level of personal distress or other motivation for therapy with a desire to implement change; (b) reasonably well-integrated personality functioning, with an ability to engage in goal-directed behaviour and some existing strengths and coping skills; and (c) some capacity to express and reflect on one's own experiences. In describing a potential client's capability of receiving real benefit and personal growth from psychoanalytically oriented psychotherapy, Coltart (1988) added that such an individual should ideally be psychologically minded.

To the extent that a young offender meets these requirements therapy would focus initially on having him relate the specifics of his offending behaviour and take responsibility for his actions. The demonstration of genuine remorse for his actions, including the expression of guilt and concern and a desire to be reparative are positive indicators for his capacity to implement change.

Given that the young person experiences distress he will have a degree of willingness to explore his thoughts and feelings and to be open to interpretations of how these events are related to his offending behaviour. By sharing memories of his childhood experiences including his past victimization, and by responding to questions, confrontations and interpretations, the client will come to understand the impact his early trauma has had on him and how it is connected to his present behaviour. Exploration and introspection will bring with it significant and powerful emotional memories and associated longings and fears that have been kept under tight control. The therapist must continually balance support, reinforcement and encouragement with a measure of emotional neutrality and attention to the young person's strengths, skills and social supports, to avoid overwhelming the young person and to avoid the transfer of dependency needs onto the therapist.

The therapy process is invariably long-term, and realistic goals and expectations for change must be timed with efforts to build the adolescent's self-esteem. Self-knowledge must be translated into behaviour change before treatment is terminated. The discontinuance of abusive behaviour would determine success in treatment but the capacity for establishing lasting non-exploitive relationships, a consistently expanding and deepening set of values and morals and self-understanding would reflect the achievement of personal identity and the readiness to confront life's demands in an adaptive way.

There is presently a dearth of research studies on psychotherapy outcome with this particular clinical population. This reflects, in part, the general tendency for these offenders to deny their acts even if they have faced charges, been found guilty and are required to attend treatment sessions according to the expectations of a period of probation (Greer & Stuart, 1983; Saunders & Awad, 1988), making them very poor candidates for individual psychodynamic therapy (Protter & Travin, 1987). Tramontana's (1980) review of psychotherapy outcome with adolescents reported that evidence does point toward the superiority of psychotherapy over no-therapy with a 75 percent positive outcome. Although Ryan and colleagues (Ryan, Lane, Davis, & Isaac, 1987) reported that psychodynamic methods would be beneficial in uncovering the origins of some of the victimized offender's adverse feelings they described individual therapy as an adjunct to group therapy methods. Kilmann, Sabalis, Gearing, Bukster, and Scovern (1982) reviewed outcome research on the treatment interventions utilized with a cross section of sexual paraphilias, including sexually abusive behaviour and reported that most publications involved case studies and the ones that did employ individual psychotherapy most often used other methods of treatment as well. They concluded that a multiple behavioural treatment package specifically tailored to aspects of the individual's arousal pattern was the most beneficial approach. Protter and Travin (1987) agreed with this finding in part but determined the most effective combination of treatments was an integrated cognitive-behavioural and focused psychodynamic paradigm with attention paid to the sexual fantasies involved in maintaining the paraphilia. McConaghy and colleagues (McConaghy, Blaszczynski, Armstrong, & Kidson, 1989) examined the adolescent sex offender's resistance to treatment and concluded that young persons treated with cognitive-behavioural and/or psycho-pharmacological interventions may be less responsive to treatment than adult offenders due to the powerful influence of hormonal control over their sexual urges. This finding is based on two studies and included six adolescents, three of whom were charged for further sexual offences. This is hardly a representative sample from which to draw conclusions that effectively relieves the offender of personal responsibility.

Although some reports of outcome statistics regarding treatment of this clinical population imply that group therapy alone is an effective treatment modality (Lombardo & DiGiorgio-Miller, 1989; Margolin, 1983; Smets & Cebula, 1987), most authors recommend a treatment program that is specifically tailored to the young offender's needs and they include individual psychotherapy as a beneficial adjunct (Groth, Hobson, Lucey, & St. Pierre, 1981; Kahn & Lafond, 1988; Rowe, 1988; Ryan et al., 1987; Saunders & Awad, 1988).

SOCIAL LEARNING MODELS

Concepts and Hypotheses

Social learning theory has been referred to as a cognitive-behaviourist (Gross & Levin, 1987) and a socio-behaviourist (Muuss, 1988) approach to the understanding of human behaviour. Given that it draws on concepts, hypotheses and methodology from many different sources, it might best be defined as an eclectic approach; however, whether one emphasizes the cognitive events that mediate the impact of external events or not, will influence both the understanding of complex human behaviours and the treatment decisions and strategies of intervention.

The common thread that appears to run through all social learning accounts of behaviour is the belief that environmental, social and situational factors, not biological and maturational factors, are responsible for development and learning. In terms of treatment it is the application of behaviouristic principles to basic developmental and social difficulties rather than exploration of intrapersonal variables that is agreed to be most effacacious.

Both factors of social learning theory recognize the importance of the young person's parents and peers as agents of socialization in the learning and maintenance of interpersonal behaviours. The cognitive theorists, however, give more credence to the self as a dispenser of rewards such that self-talk and the personal experience of pleasure serve to reinforce patterns of behaviour. The socio-behaviourists, on the other hand, believe behaviour to be governed almost exclusively by external sources including the broader spectrum of cultural and societal expectations.

For clear understanding of the young sex offender who has himself been victimized as a child, the cognitive-behaviourist wants to know the meaning the child has ascribed to his victimization and the things he says to himself about that experience. The socio-behaviourist puts more emphasis on the impact of the model and what that person represents in terms of reinforcement, as well as specific social reinforcers for the maintenance of the offending behaviour pattern.

The relationship between the young offender and his perpetrator is important information in terms of understanding the significance of the young person's offending behaviour, and the strength of the sequence of events that lead to offending for both theorists.

Imitation of a model's behaviour is most likely to occur if that person is perceived by the child to be attractive, prestigious, competent, and/or powerful; if the model is the dispenser of rewards, either monetary or emotional; and if the model is of the same gender. Based on these premises it seem clear that if the adolescent's offender was the father or father-figure, the chances of sexually abusive behaviour being imitated by the victim are high. That young males are victims of sexual offences at the hands of their fathers more often than might have been thought is not a new idea (Cooper & Cormier, 1982; Dixon, Arnold, & Calestro, 1978) but lack of reporting for numerous reasons (Finkelhor, 1984; Nasjleti, 1986) makes this a less visible social issue.

Principles of social learning theory would seem to dictate that the young offender, in imitating learned and reinforced behaviour, would choose young male victims. In explaining female victims these theorists underscore the importance of cognition and agents of social control that might influence the young offender's choice of victims. Variables of self-control or lack thereof, are also regarded to be significant factors in the repetition of behaviour patterns.

The duration of the young offender's own victimization is important insofar as learning becomes more ingrained with frequency of exposure. For the young offender who was victimized on one occasion the socio-behaviourist might include the possible frustration of dependency hypothesis to explain imitative behaviour. That is, impairment in the development of healthy dependency relationship with the parents may directly or indirectly contribute to feelings of hostility and aggression such that the young person performs sexually aggressive acts that he has been subjected to, however infrequently. The behaviour is maintained either by virtue of thought processes and self-statements, the reinforcement of sexual pleasure, or by the social support system. Awad, Saunders, and Levene's (1984) finding that the adolescent sex offender is more similar to, than different from, the juvenile non-sex offender would support this notion.

The type of sexual activity to which the adolescent was exposed will, according to this theory, have a bearing on the acts he performs as an offender. There is support in the literature to suggest that the sexual offences of some individuals are the repetition of those behaviours to which the offender was subjected (Groth, 1979). To explain those actions committed by the young offender that he was not a victim of, social learning theorists draw on other agents of social control that have introduced significantly powerful, attractive models of influence. The behaviour and expectations of the young person's peer culture (Muuss, 1988), the male socialization process (Herman, 1984), and exposure to pornography (Burgess, 1984) have all been implicated as significant to the young person's learning of antisocial or otherwise aberrant sexual behaviours. Kearns and Nutter's (1988) recent study of the pornography experience of adult sex offenders, paraphiliacs, sexual dysfunction patients, and controls does not support this hypothesis with findings of no differences between groups; however, results based on a heterogeneous sample of adult offenders cannot be generalized to adolescent offenders who have themselves been victimized.

The degree of physical aggression or force used against the young person speaks to the issue of dangerousness regarding future sexual acting-out behaviour. The more force the young person experienced as a victim the more force he would be predicted to employ as an offender. Even if the adolescent did not observe the use of violence or aggression as a victim, if he is witness to other forms of intrafamilial aggression, is encouraged by his parents to use forceful means outside the home to get his needs met and/or is subject to the frustration of dependency needs, increased aggressive behaviour toward potential victims would be predicted. The possibility that non-contact sexual crimes might escalate to more serious sexual assaults has been investigated with adult sexual offenders (Longo & Groth, 1983). These researchers found that this is the case for many sexual offenders. Identifying cognitive and self-reinforcing factors as important contributors to the link between cognition and behaviour, MacCulloch and colleagues (MacCulloch, Snowden, Wood, & Mills (1983) found in their psychopathic adult sample of male in-patients that repetitive sadistic masturbatory fantasies "had spilled over into overt behaviour because the patients had felt impelled to seek and create increasingly dangerous in vivo 'try-outs' of their fantasies" (p. 20). The findings highlight the significance of cognitive factors related to performance of behaviour regarding adolescents despite the fact that the study examined adult offenders. It might be argued that sexual fantasies accompanied by reinforcing principles of self-stimulation are more common among young offenders given their heightened sexual impulses and their lack of available, willing sexual partners.

Intervention

Cognitive-behavioural therapists are likely to use any one, or any combination of several different treatment interventions to modify the young offender's sexually inappropriate behaviours and to alter incorrect thinking patterns that precede sexually abusive actions. The socio-behaviourist is apt to employ treatment techniques that modify the reinforcing properties of aberrant sexual activity.

In terms of encouraging the young person to admit to his offending behaviour, group therapy is a popular strategy (Davis &Leitenberg, 1987) since one of the functions of denial is to protect one's self from being rejected by others. In a group of other young offenders the client will be less threatened by fears of social ridicule and peer rejection and will be encouraged by other members to own up to his crime.

The tendency for sex offenders to deny responsibility even when they have admitted their actions is relatively common (Kahn & Lafond, 1988) and group members can be influential in stopping the young person from projecting blame in an atmosphere that is supportive but places some expectations on all group members. The finding that individuals who express aggressive and other externalizing antisocial behaviours have not internalized adequate empathic responses to inhibit their actions (Miller & Eisenberg, 1988) has encouraged group therapists to teach these individuals care and concern for others by the use of peer interaction, role taking and collective behaviour methods (Margolin, 1983). The group modality has also been successfully employed with psychiatric male adolescent non-sex offenders for the self-control of anger and aggressive behaviour (Feindler, Ecton, Kingsley, & Dubey, 1986) and would seem to be appropriate to modify the behaviour of aggressive sexual offenders as well.

In terms of sensitizing the young offender to the chain of events that result in sexual acting-out, Ryan and colleagues (Ryan et al., 1987) have presented a model of the sexual assault cycle that utilizes cognitive-behavioural methods to help the young person understand the cognitive, behavioural, situational, and psychological factors that lead to sexual abuse. The intervention strategy is employed within a group modality and individual therapy is recommended as an adjunct. Cognitive restructuring has been advocated as an effective technique for altering distorted beliefs associated with childhood abuse (Jehu, Klassen, & Gazan, 1986). The significance of these patterns of thinking as related to the current offending behaviours and the client's overall level of self-esteem cannot be overstated, and the recognition of erroneous thought patterns might help the adolescent become aware of other instances of self-talk that contribute to sexual acting-out.

The development of alternative modes of self-expression, need gratification and impulse management for these young offenders is the ultimate goal of any treatment program and will be more or less successful depending on a number of important factors: (a) the individual's existing strengths and adaptive coping skills; (b) the quantity and quality of support and understanding that is being provided by family members, especially parents; (c) the client's willingness to implement change; (d) the length of time the adolescent has been engaging in maladaptive patterns of thinking and acting on sexual thoughts and impulses; and (e) the young client's motivation to take part in any kind of intervention program.

CONCLUSION

The young male sex offender who has been subjected to childhood sexual abuse represents a special concern to the therapist involved in his treatment. From both the psychodynamic and social learning perspectives, the young person's victimization represents a significant treatment issue; however, the implications for dealing with that historical fact differ between these two theoretical camps. Both agree that he has been taught to behave in highly maladaptive, potentially very dangerous ways, and that he has been reinforced at some level for this behaviour. The psychodynamic psychotherapist views the historical abuse as the main treatment issue in some ways. Although he/she is cognizant of, and monitors risk factors regarding potential acting-out, the focus of intervention will include the past trauma and the effects this experience has had on the adolescent's current functioning. This exploratory method is both a strength and a weakness of this model. The strength lies in the attention to the unmet needs of the abused child and the healing of those emotional wounds that allow the young adolescent to begin to feel better about himself and develop more effective skills of coping as a result of a more integrated sense of self. The weakness of this model's therapeutic approach is that introspection and exploration of past traumas must be carefully balanced against the client's ability to employ healthy ways of coping with increased levels of stress associated with painful memories. The process of exploration might well precipitate a sexually abusive act.

The social learning perspective offers some relatively short-term interventions that have been found to be successful with some young offenders and the direct attention paid to cognitions as related to abusive behaviours is a definite strength of this model. The weakness seems to be in the lack of attention given to effects on the past trauma in establishing deep-seated emotional conflict and identity crises.

As has been outlined, both models address the issues and goals of working with this difficult population. The most beneficial treatment program would be a combination of psychodynamic and social learning approaches specifically designed to meet the needs of the individual young offender.

REFERENCES

Ageton, S. (1983). *Sexual assault among adolescents.* Lexington, MA: Lexington Books, D.C. Heath & Company.

American Psychological Association. (1981). Ethical principles of psychologists. *American Psychologists, 36,* 633–638.

Awad, G.A., Saunders, E., & Levine, J. (1984). A clinical study of male adolescent sexual offenders. *International Journal of Offender Therapy and Comparative Criminology, 28,* 105–116.

Becker, J.V., Kaplan, M.S., Cunningham-Rathner, J., & Kavoussi, R. (1986). Characteristics of adolescent incest sexual perpetrators: Preliminary findings. *Journal of Family Violence, 1*(1), 85–97.

Breer, W. (1987). *The adolescent molester.* Springfield, IL: Charles C. Thomas.

Burgess, A.W. (1984). *Child pornography and sex rings.* Lexington, MA: Lexington Books, D.C. Heath & Company.

Burgess, A.W., Hartman, C.R., & McCormack, A. (1987). Abused to abuser: Antecedents of socially deviant behaviors. *American Journal of Psychiatry, 144*, 1431–1436.

Canadian Psychological Association, Committee on Ethics. (1986a). Code of ethics. *Highlights, 8*(1), 6E–12E.

Canadian Psychological Association, (1986b). Code of ethics. *Highlights, 8*(2), 2E.

Coltart, N.E.C. (1988). The assessment of psychological mindedness in the Diagnostic Interview. *British Journal of Psychiatry, 153*, 819–820.

Cooper, I., & Cormier, B.M. (1982). Inter-generational transmission of incest. *Canadian Journal of Psychiatry, 27*, 231–235.

Davis, G.E., & Leitenberg, H. (1987). Adolescent sex offenders. *Psychological Bulletin, 101*, 417–427.

Dixon, K.N., Arnold, E., & Calestro, K. (1978). Father-son incest: Underreported psychiatric problem? *American Journal of Psychiatry, 135*, 835–838.

Emans, R.L. (1988). Psychology's responsibility in false accusations of child abuse. *Journal of Clinical Psychology, 44*, 1000–1004.

Fehrenbach, P.A., & Monastersky, C. (1988). Characteristics of female adolescent sexual offenders. *American Journal of Orthopsychiatry, 58*(1), 148–151.

Feindler, E.L., Ecton, R.B., Kingsley, D., & Dubey, D. (1986). Group anger-control training for institutionalized psychiatric male adolescents. *Behavioral Therapy, 17*, 109–123.

Finkelhor, D. (1984). *Child sexual abuse: New theory and research.* New York: Free Press.

Finkelhor, D., & Browne, A. (1985). The traumatic impact of child sexual abuse: A conceptualization. *American Journal of Orthopsychiatry, 55*, 530–539.

Freeman-Longo, R.E. (1986). The impact of sexual victimization on males. *Child Abuse and Neglect, 10*, 411–414.

Greer, J.G., & Stuart, I.R. (Eds.). (1983). *The sexual aggressor: Current perspectives on treatment.* New York: Van Nostrand Reinhold.

Gross, A.M., & Levin, R.B. (1987). Learning. In V.B. Van Hasselt & M. Hersen (Eds.), *Handbook of adolescent psychology.* (pp. 77–90). New York: Pergamon.

Groth, A.N. (1978). Guidelines for the assessment and management of the offender. In A.W. Burgess, A.N. Groth, L.L. Holmstrom & S. Sgroi (Eds.), *Sexual assault of children and adolescents* (pp. 25–42). Lexington, MA: Lexington Books, D.C. Heath & Company.

Groth, A.N. (1979). Sexual trauma in the life histories of rapists and child molesters. *Victimology: An International Journal, 4*(1), 10–16.

Groth, A.N., & Hobson, W.F. (1983). The dynamics of sexual assault. In L. B. Schlesinger & E. Revitch (Eds.), *Sexual dynamics of anti-social behavior* (pp. 159–172). Springfield, IL: Charles C. Thomas.

Groth, A.N., Hobson, W.F., & Gary, T.S. (1982). The child molester: Clinical observations. In J. Conte & D.A. Shore (Eds.), *Social work and child sexual abuse* (pp. 129–144). New York: Haworth Press.

Groth, A.N., Hobson, W.F., Lucey, K.P., & St. Pierre, J. (1981). Juvenile sexual offenders: Guidelines for treatment. *International Journal of Offender Therapy and Comparative Criminology, 25*(3), 265–272.

Handy, L.C., & Cammaert, L.P. (1985). *Power: A major construct of child sexual abuse.* Paper presented at the meeting of the Canadian Psychological Association. Halifax, Nova Scotia.

Herman, J. (1984). Colloquium: Sexual Violence. *Work in Progress. Stone Center for Developmental Services and Studies.* No. 83–05. Wellesley, MA.

Jehu, D., Klassen, C., & Gazan, M. (1986). Cognitive restructuring of distorted beliefs associated with childhood sexual abuse. In J. Gripton & M. Valentich (Eds.), *Social work practice in sexual problems* (pp. 49–69). London: Haworth Press.

Kahn, T.J., & Lafond, M.A. (1988). Treatment of the adolescent sexual offender. *Child and Adolescent Social Work, 5*(2), 135–148.

Kearns, C.M., & Nutter, D.E. (1988). A preliminary examination of the pornography experience of sex offenders, paraphiliacs, sexual dysfunction patients, and controls based on Meese Commission recommendations. *Journal of Sex and Marital Therapy, 14*, 284–298.

Kemp, J.A., & Williams, D. (Eds.). (1982). *Sexual abuse of children conference.* Winnipeg, MA: Department of the Attorney General.

Kilmann, P.R., Sabalis, R.F., Gearing, M.L., II, Bukster, L.H., & Scovern, A.W. (1982). The treatment of sexual paraphilias: A review of the outcome research. *The Journal of Sex Research, 18*(3), 193–252.

Lerner, H. (1987). Psychodynamic models. In V.B. Van Hasselt & M. Hersen (Eds.), *Handbook of adolescent psychology* (pp. 53–76). New York: Pergamon.

Lewis, D.O., Shanok, S.S., & Pincus, J.H. (1981). Juvenile male sexual assaulters: Psychiatric, neurological, psychoeducational, and abuse factors. In D.O. Lewis (Ed.), *Vulnerabilities to delinquency* (pp. 89–105). New York: Spectrum.

Lombardo, R., & DiGiorgio-Miller, J. (1989). Concepts and techniques in working with juvenile sex offenders. *Journal of Offender Counseling, Services and Rehabilitation, 13*(1), 39–53.

Longo, R.E., & Groth, A.N. (1983). Juvenile sexual offenses in the histories of adult rapists and child molesters. *International Journal of Offender Therapy and Comparative Criminology, 27*, 150–155.

MacCulloch, M.J., Snowden, P.R., Wood, P.J.W., & Mills, H.E. (1983). Sadistic fantasy, sadistic behavior and offending. *British Journal of Psychiatry, 143*, 20–29.

Mantell, D.M. (1988). Clarifying erroneous child sexual abuse allegations. *American Journal of Orthopsychiatry, 58*, 618–621.

Margolin, L. (1983). A treatment model for the adolescent sex offender. *Journal of Offender Counseling, Services and Rehabilitation, 8*(1/2), 1–12.

McConaghy, N., Blaszczynski, A., Armstrong, M.S., & Kidson, W. (1989). Resistance to treatment of adolescent sex offenders. *Archives of Sexual Behavior, 18*(2), 97–107.

Miller, P.A., & Eisenberg, N. (1988). The relation of empathy to aggressive and externalizing antisocial behavior. *Psychological Bulletin, 103*, 324–344.

Muuss, R.E. (1988). *Theories of adolescence* (5th ed.) New York: Random House.

Nasjleti, M. (1986). Suffering in silence: The male incest victim. In D.C. Haden (Ed.), *Out of harm's way: Readings on child sexual abuse: Its prevention and treatment* (pp. 66–71). Phoenix, AZ: Oryx Press.

Protter, B., & Travin, S. (1987). Sexual fantasies in the treatment of paraphiliac disorder: A bimodal approach. *Psychiatric Quarterly, 58*, 279–297.

Rowe, B. (1988). Practical treatment of adolescent sexual offenders. *Journal of Child Care, 3*(6), 51–58.

Ryan, G., Lane, S., Davis, J., & Isaac, C. (1987). Juvenile sex offenders: Development and correction. *Child Abuse and Neglect, 11*, 385–395.

Saunders, E., & Awad, G. (1988). Assessment, management, and treatment planning for male adolescent sexual offenders. *American Journal of Orthopsychiatry, 58*, 571–579.

Seghorn, T., Prentky, R.A., & Boucher, R.J. (1987). Childhood sexual abuse in the lives of sexually aggressive offenders. *American Academy of Child and Adolescent Psychiatry, 26*, 262–267.

Smets, A.C., & Cebula, C.M. (1987). A group treatment program for adolescent sex offenders: Five steps toward resolution. *Child Abuse and Neglect, 11*, 247–254.

Tramontana, M.G. (1980). Critical review of research on psychotherapy outcome with adolescents: 1967–1977. *Psychological Bulletin, 88*, 429–450.

Waterman, J., & Lusk, R. (1986). Scope of the problem. In K. MacFarlane, J. Waterman, S. Conerly, L. Damon, M. Durfee & S. Long (Eds.), *Sexual abuse of young children* (pp. 3–12). New York: Guilford.

Weiner, I.B. (1976). Individual psychotherapy. In I.B. Weiner (Ed.), *Clinical methods in psychology* (pp. 333–391). New York: Wiley.

Yates, A., & Musty, T. (1988). Preschool children's erroneous allegations of sexual molestation. *American Journal of Psychiatry, 145*, 989–992.

JOURNAL OF CHILD AND YOUTH CARE SPECIAL ISSUE PAGES 103 – 128

DEVELOPMENT AND EVALUATION OF A FAMILY SYSTEMS APPROACH TO THE TREATMENT OF CHILD SEXUAL ABUSE

ROBBIE BABINS-WAGNER[1]
FACULTY OF SOCIAL WORK, THE UNIVERSITY OF CALGARY

Abstract: The development of a unique family systems program, located within a general hospital, for the treatment of families in which a member has been sexually abused by a member of that family is described. While the program is based on the therapeutic models and insights of Larson and Maddock, it has developed uniquely important features, including comprehensive clinical assessments before a family is admitted to the program, and assessments to measure program outcomes. This program works in cooperation with child welfare programs in both protecting and serving the needs of children.

PROGRAM PHILOSOPHY

The Family Sexual Abuse Treatment Program (FSATP) described in this paper is the first program in Western Canada to provide service to victims of child sexual abuse through a family systems-oriented treatment process. Victims and offenders, together with other family members, are treated conjointly from the onset of the treatment process. Individual counselling is not usually provided prior to the first family meeting.

A family-systems approach for the treatment of sexual abuse utilized by the FSATP is a new and innovative method of treatment. It differs from other family treatment programs (Giarretto, 1982) in that victims, offenders and spouses are seen together from the onset of treatment without prior individual or group treatment. The basic pre-condition to utilizing this model is the completion of an extensive Diagnostic Evaluation which includes clinical interview data, objective testing data, as well as collateral data, in order to select clients for the program. *Not all clients referred to the FSATP are selected for treatment.* The FSATP works with families which best fit an intensive family model and refers clients not accepted for treatment to other treatment programs in Calgary, better suited to the particular family's needs.

The FSATP was developed in 1986 in response to child welfare needs to provide additional treatment services to victims of child sexual abuse and their families. The FSATP responds to Alberta Family and Social

Services' focus on strengthening the family in order to prevent or reduce the extensive use of government intervention in the care for children. This is accomplished by utilizing a family systems approach to assessment and treatment which allows for potentially reducing child welfare intervention, keeping families intact if the family chooses to remain together, helping families separate if that is the direction they choose to move towards, or assisting families, so that they can make the necessary changes to reduce child welfare involvement.

The FSATP enables the reduction of child welfare intervention by facilitating the necessary changes in client families so as to decrease the possibility of the sexual abuse recurring in the future.

To this end, the FSATP supports the following principles:

- Sexual abuse often involves the entire nuclear family system and frequently the extended family network.
- Sexual abuse can sometimes be viewed as a symptom of family disorganization or dysfunction.
- Sexual abuse, as a symptom, can develop as a patterned attempt to do something positive for the system.
- Symptoms can be signals that needs for autonomy and differentiation are being sacrificed in order to maintain dysfunctional family relationships.
- Personality and behaviour are not only attributes of individuals, but are characteristics which develop through repeated interactions and experiences.
- One part of the assessment may focus on understanding the function of the symptom within the family system.
- The focus of treatment is on interactions between family members.
- Victims of sexual abuse are often treated in the context of the family, but may also be seen individually.
- Treatment can be family-systems oriented or victim-advocacy oriented, depending upon the needs of a particular family.
- Treatment is change and action oriented — thus emphasizing behaviour change.
- A systemic strategic understanding of sexual abuse allows for an integration of treatment modalities that includes individually focused and family focused approaches with no inherent conflict.

The FSATP is based on the suggestion by Larson and Maddock (1986) that sexually abusive behaviour fulfills different functions in different families. Four functions or categories have been identified: CATEGORY I – affection exchange; CATEGORY II – erotic exchange; CATEGORY III – aggression exchange; and CATEGORY IV – expression of rage. The categories, while sufficiently well defined to allow for the categorization of families, are not mutually exclusive and are perceived as lying on a continuum. (Table 1). The left most end of the continuum (Category I type cases) corresponds approximately with the philosophy of the Child Abuse Movement; that is, intrafamilial sexual abuse is seen as a symptom of family dysfunction to which all family members have made some contribution. Treatment, therefore, is focused on family therapy with the aim of assisting the family in the resolution of these problems or dysfunctions. The right most end of the continuum corresponds to the feminist view that sexual abuse should be identified with rape and is viewed, not as a symptom of family dysfunction, but as a product of patriarchal social structure and male socialization.

The treatment goal here is to empower the mother to protect the victim in the continued absence of the offender. FSATP attempts to effect a compromise between these views while giving credence to both. Following the typology suggested by Larson and Maddock, families are placed into one of the four categories after the assessment, and treatment is planned according to the function which the sexual abuse appears to fill. The strategic/systemic family therapy offered by the program is viewed as generally successful with Categories I and II, somewhat less successful with Category III, and unsuccessful with Category IV. Families assessed as belonging to Category IV are therefore not accepted into the program.

THEORETICAL FRAMEWORK

A. Assessment

Sexual abuse is a "distortion of the sexual dimension of family experience arising out of a complex combination of mutually influencing valuables in each of four existential" categories: Intrapsychic; Systemic; Developmental; and Situational (Maddock, 1983).

The Intrapsychic, Developmental and Situational variables have been well articulated by many authors (Groth, Hobson, & Gray, 1982; Justice & Justice, 1976; Weinberg, 1955; Finkelhor, 1979, 1984). The Systemic variables are the structural and functional variables which aid in our conceptualization of the problem of sexual abuse. These include the identification of "boundary disturbances" in four areas:

1. the boundary between the family and its social environment;
2. the boundary between adult and child generations in the family;
3. interpersonal/role boundaries between family members; and
4. intrapsychic boundaries within family members (Larson, 1980, pp. 71–72).

Sexual abuse usually occurs in a family system that is relatively closed, undifferentiated, and rigid in both structure and function, i.e., a product of substantial boundary disturbance (Larson & Maddock, 1986).

The motivation of sexual abuse offenders differs from individual to individual, just as the sexual abuse serves a different function in every family in which it occurs.

Sexual abuse is meaningful within the context in which it occurs. The meaning of the sexual abuse evolves from the particular patterns of interaction that characterize a given family: the meaning of the behaviour shared by the family members serves as the basis for further sequences of behaviour, which in turn lead to new meanings, and so on (Barton & Alexander, 1981). The function that the sexual abuse serves in a given family system arises out of the network of meanings which ties together family members and influences their patterns of interaction (Larson & Maddock, 1986).

In incest families, sexual involvement with children can be categorized as serving four basic functions involved in interperson exchange processes: affection, eroticism, aggression or the expression of rage (Larson & Maddock, 1986). When placed on a continuum and integrated with the other functional variables (Table 1), a functional typology of four categories is created which can be used for assessment and treatment planning (Larson & Maddock, 1986).

Table 1
Incest Family Typology

AFFECTION EXCHANGE PROCESS	EROTIC EXCHANGE PROCESS	AGGRESSION EXCHANGE PROCESS	EXPRESSION OF RAGE PROCESS
Positive Intent	Positive Intent	Negative Intent	Negative Intent
Object Connection	Object Connection	No Object Connection	Object Displacement
Non-violent	Non-violent	Often Violent	Violent, Life-threatening
Power Motive Minimal	Power Motive May Be Present	Power Motive Present	Power Motive Primary
Individual	Individual	Individual	Individual
Psychopathology	Psychopathology	Psychopathology	Psychopathology
Not Critical	Not Critical	May Be Critical	Critical and Primary

Category I

When the incest has been part of an affection exchange process, outpatient treatment is provided. These are cases where clients tended to be motivated for treatment and it is often recommended in these cases that the offender not be separated from the family. Interviewing and testing of members of an affectionately-based incest family may reveal some anxiety, depression, and stronger than average dependency needs.

Individual psychopathology, especially in the perpetrator, is usually not sufficient to inhibit relatively effective functioning in most areas of life.

Category II

Where the incest has been part of an erotic exchange process, outpatient treatment is again recommended. The incestuous behaviour in these families may involve both parent and children and have a "game-like" quality. Much of the focus is on teasing and titillation; violence is relatively seldom seen and family members are socialized into a pervasive erotic ambiance.

Category III

If the incest was part of an aggression exchange process, a combination of outpatient and inpatient treatment is recommended. In these families, the perpetrator may deal angrily — even violently — with the victim, and free-floating hostility is often prevalent. This intent to hurt someone via incestuous activity contrasts with the dynamics of the families described in Categories I and II in which the behaviour serves as a misguided effort at positive communication.

This aggression-based incest dynamic creates an atmosphere fostering individual psychopathology as well as a distorted family structure. There is an underlying lack of impulse control coupled with a fear of direct interpersonal conflict. Separation of offender and victim is usually necessary in these types of families.

Category IV

If the incest was part of an expression of rage process, inpatient treatment is recommended. The offender's anger is not focused, but is a primitive expression resulting from longstanding frustration. If the incestuous activity in this type of family is sudden and violent, family members may respond by reporting the event so that outsiders can intervene. However, if the abuse is episodic, family members may be more likely to "learn to live with it" and take a generalized "victim" stance toward life.

B. Treatment

The four categories described in Table 1 can serve as guidelines for developing treatment approaches that are highly compatible with both the functional meaning and the structural characteristics of various families. A fuller description of the criteria for assessment and their relationship to the treatment process can be found in Larson and Maddock (1986).

Table II provides an overview of the types of treatment indicated for families in Categories I, II, III, and IV. Once a treatment approach has been selected, the therapist will provide and coordinate all therapy for the family. Ongoing family meetings will occur throughout the course of treatment, even if family therapy is not the treatment of choice.

Table 2
Incest Family Typology Treatment Considerations

AFFECTION EXCHANGE PROCESS	EROTIC EXCHANGE PROCESS	AGGRESSION EXCHANGE PROCESS	EXPRESSION OF RAGE PROCESS
Outpatient Treatment	Outpatient Treatment	Outpatient/Inpatient Treatment	Inpatient Treatment
Family Therapy Primary	Group Therapy for Family Members Primary	Group Therapy for Family Members Primary	Individual Therapy Primary
Separation Not Necessary	Separation Sometimes Necessary	Separation Usually Necessary	Separation Necessary And Critical
Perhaps Group Therapy	Family Therapy	Family Therapy	Group Therapy
	Marital Therapy	Marital Therapy	Perhaps Family Therapy
		Perhaps Individual Therapy	Perhaps Marital Therapy
Structural/Strategic Family Approaches, Supportive Group Therapy	Confrontive, "Addiction" Group Approaches, and Structural/Strategic Family and Marital Therapy	Confrontive Group Approaches, Structural/Strategic Family and Marital Therapy, Empathic Individual Therapy	Empathic, Psycho-dynamic Individual Therapy, Supportive Group Therapy, Structural/Strategic Marital and Family Therapy

C. Methods of Intervention

Specific methods of intervention as developed by Larson and Maddock (1986) for the four kinds of incest families will be briefly outlined:

Category I
Treatment for affection-based incest families focuses explicitly on boundary issues. Family members are encouraged to function as individuals. Affiliative needs are directed toward others outside the family (for example, the formation of supportive networks). The focus for the offender is on increased self-esteem and personal identity issues.

Category II
Treatment for erotic-based incest families focuses on education, attitude change and reality testing. These families tend to have combined rigid

sexual stereotypes with role-related power struggles. Group therapy with peers is useful, particularly in the earlier stages of treatment. Marital therapy with a sexual focus is likely indicated. Living arrangements are dealt with carefully and thoroughly as erotic interaction patterns may be so well established that physical separation of the offender and victim may be necessary.

Category III

Treatment for aggression-based families focuses on education, anger management and conflict resolution. These families often require highly-controlled living situations due to their lack of impulse control and coercive sexual exploitation or violence. Family members require separation from each other during the early and middle phases of treatment. Group therapy formats need to be highly confrontive in order to help family members learn to deal creatively with anger and conflict in relationships without linking these to sex. Marital therapy emphasizes conflict management and resolution. Family therapy focuses on intergenerational power struggles and developmental issues. All aspects of treatment for family members attends to the underlying issues of shame and low self-esteem.

Category IV

Treatment for rage-based incest families is not provided by FSATP.

D. Therapeutic Issues

There is little in the literature to indicate which specific techniques are effective in treating cases of sexual abuse. Treatment activities have been drawn from the systemic/strategic family therapy literature. There is much less dependence on group therapy in this program than in many others. The FSATP is currently piloting an offender group but does not usually provide group therapy. It takes the view that clients may not need additional therapy. Participation in ordinary, age-related activities is advocated. Use is made of community resources such as the YWCA, etc.

With regard to victim groups, program staff are concerned that these groups are often too focused on the child's experience of victimization and not focused enough on normal developmental needs of the victim. Mothers, too, are often thought to be unready for the group experience which may focus on their own victimization in the relationship or bring forth memories of their victimization as children. Referrals are made, however, if the victim's or mother's own victimization is preventing her from moving on in the therapy process and the counselling being offered is not providing the support and normalization which may be offered by a group.

Offenders who require a highly confrontative approach to treatment may be referred to the forensic outpatient unit at the Calgary General

Hospital, one of the only groups offered for offenders in the Calgary region. Therapy sessions normally last between one and two hours and continue for an average of 18 months.

Client Profile

The FSATP provides treatment to cases of intrafamilial forms of sexual abuse including any form of sexual activity between a child and a parent, parent surrogate, sibling or extended family member (i.e., father, mother, aunt, uncle, common-laws, spouse, grandparent, siblings).

Adolescent offenders who have committed intra or extrafamilial abuse are seen in the context of their families. Cases of extrafamilial abuse where the offender was a babysitter, etc., are considered on an individual basis and accepted only if space permits. Victims under the age of eight are usually referred to Alberta Children's Hospital while adult survivors are referred to the Sexual Assault Center.

Present eligibility criteria for families centre around placement of the family into one of the four categories discussed earlier. Families fitting Categories I and II are accepted preferentially, Category III families are accepted if the offender is accepting responsibility for the sexual abuse, and Category IV families are not accepted.

Service Objective

The first priority of FSATP is to provide for the safety and protection of children who are referred. Program goals aim to keep the family intact, if at all possible, and/or to reintegrate the child and/or the offending parent/step-parent back into the family as soon as it is safe and feasible to do so. The primary treatment goal is to ensure that the sexual abuse does not occur again; the secondary goal is the preservation and unification of the family.

Ten specific objectives were initially developed to meet program activities. Over the past two years an additional twenty objectives have been identified which will be included in the program description in the 1991–92 fiscal year. The ten original objectives were:

1. TO ESTABLISH AN APPROPRIATE FAMILY STRUCTURE

The literature suggests that boundary problems occur in families experiencing sexual abuse. Role reversal between mother and daughter is common, unequal power relationships between males and females may exist and relationship patterns between family members may be symbiotic.

2. TO INCREASE MARITAL SATISFACTION

Family sexual abuse is often related to marital problems. Marital satisfaction may be low with tension and hostility increasing as the couple fail to meet each other's emotional needs. Marital satisfaction is not necessarily linked to sexual satisfaction.

3. TO INCREASE THE SEXUAL SATISFACTION OF THE COUPLE

Sexual dissatisfaction may be present in families where the parent looks to a child to meet intimacy needs. In other words, failure of the couple to meet each other's sexual needs may lead to sexualization of the children.

4. TO INCREASE THE SELF-ESTEEM OF FAMILY MEMBERS

When boundaries are blurred and inappropriate, affirmation of self is difficult to achieve. The couple's inability to meet each other's needs may accentuate poor self-image on their part and the victim may perceive herself/himself as "bad" both because she/he was abused and because she/he revealed the abuse.

5. TO INCREASE THE FAMILY'S COPING MECHANISMS

Strauss (1973, 1980) has suggested that sexual interaction may become a way of dealing with family stress. Since sexually abusive families are often isolated, it becomes important both to help them develop support networks and to increase their own coping skills.

6. TO ESTABLISH EFFECTIVE COMMUNICATION

If sexual abuse is viewed as a symptom of family dysfunction, it is likely that ineffective communication, which is both a cause and an effect of dysfunction, may also be present. Unclear and indirect messages may lead to diffused roles and to feelings of dissatisfaction since the needs of family members remain unexpressed and thus unmet. Instrumental communication may be emphasized with little affective communication.

7. TO CLARIFY FAMILY VALUE SYSTEMS WITH REGARD TO SEXUAL BEHAVIOUR

The sexualization of a child's need for nurturance may have become established over several generations, leading to acceptance of sexual relations between family members as the norm.

8. TO CLARIFY FAMILY MYTHS WITH REGARD TO GENDER ISSUES

Families who adhere closely to stereotypical male and female roles may experience difficulties in a society where gender issues are in a state of flux and are often a point of contention. For example, a husband who feels he should be able to support his family but is unemployed may experience feelings of shame and resentment — perhaps reinforced by the fact that his wife is working. Or husband and wife may be unable to form a parental team for the purpose of fulfilling each other's needs and nurturing their children.

9. TO CLARIFY FAMILY MYTHS WITH REGARD TO SEXUAL DEVELOPMENT

Families may not be aware of children's developmental needs or of appropriate age-related sexual behaviours. They may misunderstand children's attempts to seek nurturance.

10. TO ASSIST THE FAMILY THROUGHOUT THE COURT PROCESS

In most sexual abuse cases, the family has no previous experience with criminal charges and is dealing with the legal system for the first time. Since the trauma of the court process may prove a real impediment to therapy, the therapist has a responsibility to help the family through this process.

SERVICE COMPONENTS

A. The Diagnostic Assessment

In order to utilize Larson and Maddock's (1986) typology with FSATP families, the following Diagnostic Assessment Procedure has been developed by the Program. The Diagnostic Assessment process is as outlined beginning with the family interview (see Appendix).

All clients referred to the FSATP are initially assessed within the family context. Following the initial family session, the therapist may decide to interview individual family members or dyads in order to complete as thorough an assessment as possible.

The following factors are included in the initial clinical assessment:

Initial Clinical Assessment:

- description of disclosure duration and frequency of abuse
- nature of the sexual abuse
- family vulnerability to sexual abuse: preconditions, precipitators
- sexual abuse in family of origin
- personality factors for individual family members
- family system factors: degree of cohesion—adaptability, family structure, family style, family communication
- socio-environmental factors: attitudes toward male/female roles, tolerance towards sexuality/incest, behaviour in the community, stress, social isolation, opportunity factors, major life changes
- preconditions for offender: motivation to abuse, overcoming internal inhibitions, overcoming external inhibitions, overcoming child's resistance
- victim responses to event: behavioural responses, psychological responses, cognitive responses.

The clinical purpose of the Pre-Treatment Evaluation is to assess the offender, spouse, victim for current indicators of adjustment/pathology to be utilized in decisions and/or planning for treatment. This most resembles a traditional clinical usage of the Psychological Assessment.

The pre-treatment evaluation is one method of addressing the concerns that victim advocates often have of family-systems programs. Victim advocates believe that a family systems analysis of incestuous behaviour is too narrow. They recommend that a family systems analysis needs to be supplemented with an individual analysis of the offender which considers whether he/she has an ingrained deviant pattern of erotic preference, whether he/she has a pattern of emotional disturbances, and whether he/she has a criminal history, all of which may contribute to the incest behaviours (Finkelhor, 1986).

The pre-treatment evaluation can clearly speak on the issues described above and assist clinical staff in making appropriate treatment recommendations.

Following the completion of all initial assessment sessions and the evaluation, the case is conferenced with all relevant program and community professionals and treatment decisions are made. These decisions are made based on the criteria as outlined by Larson and Maddock (1986).

B. Treatment

Once a treatment approach has been selected, the therapist provides and coordinates all therapy for the family. Ongoing family meetings are provided throughout the course of treatment, even if family therapy is not the treatment of choice.

Treatment is carried out primarily on an outpatient basis, using the facilities at the Rockyview General Hospital. Inpatient facilities are available to the FSATP at both the Holy Cross Hospital and Rockyview General Hospital, should clients require short-term inpatient assessment and/or intervention as part of their overall treatment program. The range of services offered include assessment, individual counselling, marital and family counselling, parenting program and psycho-sexual education.

C. Other Services Offered

Services offered by the Parent and Child Treatment Program are available to FSATP clients. Additional services are developed to meet family and program needs. Clients may be referred to groups offered through other community-based programs while continuing in treatment through the FSATP.

D. Coordination of Services

Coordination of services in the FSATP is considered within the hospital system and in relation to Alberta Family and Social Services (AFSS). Within the hospital, it is the role of the prime therapist to coordinate treatment services for the client and/or family system. This is done to ensure that treatment goals and plans are being met and that clients are not referred to too many services at any one time. It is the therapist's role to liaise with FSATP staff, inpatient staff and other professionals, when necessary.

The prime therapist also has the responsibility to liaise and communicate with AFSS. The relationship between Child Welfare and FSATP staff is crucial. Program staff must know that they will have AFSS support regarding assessment and treatment. The family must clearly know that Child Welfare is the authority and is recommending treatment for the family.

Decisions about removal of the offender or child are made conjointly by the FSATP and Child Welfare workers once treatment has begun. The child's need to be protected is of primary importance. The prime therapist communicates directly with the Child Welfare worker to complete assessments and provide treatment recommendations. It is expected that the Child Welfare worker attend the case conference where the case is discussed. Child Welfare workers are invited to view family, individual, or couple sessions whenever possible as one way of being informed about progress in the case. Child Welfare workers are asked to communicate crises to FSATP and to allow program staff to work through the crisis with the family. The FSATP requests that Child Welfare not close files until at least the initial case conference unless agreed upon earlier by both FSATP staff and Child Welfare.

It is crucial that only one person communicate with Child Welfare and other involved professionals in order to minimize confusion for the clients.

E. Education and Training

FSATP staff provide practicums to students from The University of Calgary from a variety of disciplines including Social Work and Nursing. Training in the FSATP's theoretical framework is provided to professional groups on a request basis. The FSATP has the objective of developing a professional training program over the next 12–18 months in order to meet the increasing number of requests for this service.

Program Activities

For each objective, specific activities or techniques derived from the literature are used to obtain the desired effect. A list of objectives with related activities follows.

Objective: To establish an appropriate family structure.
Activities:
1. Modelling
2. Stimulating gossip in the presence of dyads, triads, or individuals
3. Tracking behavioural sequences
4. Specification of parent-child boundaries
5. Active listening
6. Apology session
7. Paradoxical intervention, e.g., hierarchical reversal
8. Assignment of in-session or out-session tasks such as letters, art, or a journal

9. Therapeutic opinion, e.g., split opinion, positive reframing
10. Cognitive restructuring such as story telling, use of metaphors, clarifying maladaptive cycles and normalization
11. Externalization of problem(s)
12. Circular questioning
13. Identifying, through family discussion, what made the family vulnerable to sexual abuse
14. Creating a hierarchy between parents and children by helping parents to become a team
15. Structural shifts (e.g., changing family composition in room)

Objective: To increase marital satisfaction
Activities:

1. Assignment of homework (e.g., writing up a list of what each member of the couple expects)
2. Active listening
3. Modelling
4. Stimulating gossip in the presence of the spouse
5. Tracking behavioural sequences
6. Paradoxical intervention
7. Therapeutic opinion, e.g., split opinion, positive reframing
8. Cognitive restructuring
9. Specification of personal boundaries, e.g., parents locking bedroom door for privacy
10. Circular questioning
11. Posing dilemmas and behavioural changes by role reversals
12. Clarifying interpersonal perception with affect or cognitive queries
13. Guide couple to reassess their commitment to each other
14. Use of rituals
15. Identifying, through discussion, what made family vulnerable to sexual abuse
16. Clarifying gender issues
17. Mediation

Objective: To increase the sexual satisfaction of the couple
Activities:

1. Assignment of homework including reading; problem-solving strategies to practice
2. Stimulating gossip in the presence of the spouse
3. Tracking behavioural sequences
4. Specification of personal boundaries
5. Active listening
6. Paradoxical intervention
7. Therapeutic opinion: split opinion, positive reframing
8. Cognitive restructuring

9. Externalization of problem
10. Circular questioning
11. Stimulating discussion on what made the couple vulnerable to family sexual abuse
12. Clarifying marital roles, expectations and beliefs
13. Providing education to the couple to clarify myths and beliefs

Objectives: To increase the self-esteem of family members

Activities:

1. Therapeutic opinion
2. Cognitive restructuring, e.g., correcting misconception that individual has of him or herself
3. Active listening
4. Modelling
5. Tracking behavioural sequences
6. Encouraging clear hierarchy for parents to be in positions of caregivers and disciplinarians
7. Assignment of in-session and out-of-session homework
8. Specification of personal boundaries
9. Externalization of the problem
10. Circular questioning
11. Referral to self-help groups for perpetrators, spouse and victim to help them normalize their feelings and for reality testing
12. Acknowledging the differences of each member's contribution to the family
13. Using family member's feedback to support other members' positive behaviours
14. Identifying through family discussion what made the family vulnerable to sexual abuse in order to diffuse blame away from victim

Objective: To increase the family's coping mechanisms

Activities:

1. Modelling
2. Stimulating gossip in the presence of dyads, triads or individuals
3. Specification of personal and parent-child boundaries
4. Active listening
5. Paradoxical intervention
6. Assignment of in-session and out-of-session tasks
7. Therapeutic opinion
8. Cognitive restructuring
9. Externalization of the problem
10. Circular questioning
11. Referral to group therapy as an opportunity to meet others in similar situations who could provide support
12. Directing affiliative needs outside the home by referrals and/or suggestions and/or encouragement to participate in community organizations

13. Guiding family towards problem-solving strategies by: role plays, modelling, partializing the problem, setting up an action plan and division of tasks
14. Crisis counselling
15. Tracking behavioural sequences and clarifying maladaptive cycle
16. Creating a hierarchy between parents and child by helping parents become a team
17. Clarifying the family roles and norms that determine the hierarchy between members
18. Coordinating advocating on behalf of the family with other systems to provide instrumental necessities

Objective: To establish effective communication

Activities:

1. Modelling
2. Therapeutic opinion
3. Cognitive restructuring
4. Active listening
5. Stimulating gossip
6. Tracking behavioural sequences and clarifying maladaptive cycles
7. Paradoxical intervention
8. Assignment of in-session and out-of-session tasks
9. Externalization of problem
10. Circular questioning
11. Confrontation
12. Focusing on individual affect, fear/anxiety, sadness/depression, etc., to be shared with family members
13. Redirecting messages to the members for whom they are intended
14. Repunctuation of events
15. Identifying, through family discussion, what made the family vulnerable to sexual abuse
16. Structural shifts, e.g., family composition in room changed

Objective: To clarify the family's value system with regard to sexual behaviour

Activities:

1. Assignment of tasks, e.g., rituals
2. Therapeutic opinions
3. Confrontation used by therapist
4. Circular questioning
5. Stimulating gossip
6. Tracking behavioural sequences
7. Specification of parent-child boundaries
8. Active listening
9. Cognitive restructuring, such as storytelling, metaphors, clarifying maladaptive cycles and normalization

10. Externalization of problem
11. Circular questioning
12. Promoting discussion of family's value system to determine information gaps or misconceptions on age appropriate sexual behaviour
13. Identifying what made the family vulnerable to sexual abuse
14. Creating a hierarchy between parents and child by helping parents become a team
15. Clarifying family roles and norms that determine hierarchy between members
16. Apology session

Objective: To clarify family myths with regard to gender issues
Activities:
1. Modelling
2. Stimulating gossip
3. Tracking behavioural sequences and clarifying maladaptive cycle
4. Active listening
5. Paradoxical intervention
6. Assignment of tasks
7. Therapeutic opinion
8. Cognitive restructuring
9. Externalization of problem
10. Circular questioning

Objective: To clarify family myths with regard to sexual development
Activities:
1. Stimulating gossip
2. Tracking behavioural sequences
3. Specification of parent-child boundaries
4. Active listening
5. Assignment of tasks
6. Therapeutic opinion
7. Cognitive restructuring
8. Circular questioning
9. Identifying what made the family vulnerable to sexual abuse

Objective: To assist the family throughout the court process
Activities:
1. Active listening
2. Crisis intervention
3. Negotiating with the family and legal counsel the topics to be addressed in therapy until the legal process is completed
4. Normalizing the family experiences
5. Providing emotional support

6. Encouraging/facilitating family members supporting each other through the court process

Termination

The decision of whether to stop treatment is crucial, as the program goal is to stop future sexual abuse within the family. The decision will be discussed with family members and the Child Welfare worker assigned to the family (if the Child Welfare file is still open) before any formal termination process occurs. The four major reasons possible for termination of treatment are:

1. Sufficient progress of the family has been made indicating decreased risk of further abuse to the children.
2. Progress is not being made and it is felt that alternative resources may better meet the family's needs.
3. The family refuses to continue therapy.
4. The family moves outside the jurisdiction of the FSATP.

Termination is discussed with the family and other involved professionals before any formal termination process is set in motion. If agreement is reached, the family is asked to participate in post-treatment evaluation. The therapist writes a discharge report at the end of treatment. An Evaluation of Services questionnaire is mailed to the family after termination in order to assess the client's perception of the effectiveness of the program.

Post-treatment Evaluation

The evaluation battery administered at the onset of treatment is also completed by clients at the end of treatment. One additional measure is added. An Evaluation of Services Questionnaire. (See Appendix 1 for Pre- and Post-Treatment Measure Descriptions.)

Follow-up

Follow-up procedures were developed and piloted in the summer of 1990. Initial feedback is not yet available.

Link Between Anticipated Results and Activities

The program's objectives, together with the linkages between objectives and activities, have been discussed in the treatment section of the report. No information is available as to what unanticipated results might have followed from the program's activities.

PROGRAM OUTCOME

Measurement of Results

Program outcome is assessed in three ways:

1. Therapist evaluation as presented in the progress and discharge reports.
2. Client satisfaction as indicated by the Client Satisfaction form completed after termination.
3. Results of the battery of measures which comprise the pre- and post-test evaluation.

In addition, the degree to which each objective was achieved is measured separately, as follows:

Objective: To establish an appropriate family structure
Measurements:
1. FACES III Scale, administered pre- and post-treatment to all family members 12 years of age or older.
2. Olsen's Clinical Rating Scale.
3. Client verbal report recorded by therapist after relevant sessions on the therapy interview form.
4. Therapist Discharge Summary

Objective: To increase the marital satisfaction of the couple
Measurements:
1. Index of Marital Satisfaction
2. Client verbal reports
3. Therapist Discharge Summary

Objective: To increase the sexual satisfaction of the couple
Measurements:
1. Index of Sexual Satisfaction
2. Client verbal reports
3. Therapist Discharge Summary

Objective: To increase the self-esteem of family members
Measurements:
1. Coopersmith Self-Esteem Scales, administered to all family members, nine years old or older
2. Client verbal reports
3. Reports from outside resources involved with family members, e.g., school report
4. Therapist Discharge Summary

Objective: To improve the family's coping mechanisms
Measurements:
1. Family Inventory of Life Events and Changes (FILE)
2. Client verbal reports
3. Therapist Discharge Summary

Objective: To establish effective communication
Measurements:
1. Parent-adolescent Communication Scale, administered to all family members 14 years old and older

2. Olsen's Clinical Rating Scale
3. The communication component of the FACES III Scale
4. Family Environment Scale, administered to all family members 12 years old and older
5. Client verbal reports
6. Therapist Discharge Summary

Objective: To clarify the family's value system with regard to sexual behaviour

Measurements:

1. Client verbal report
2. Therapist Discharge Summary

Objective: To clarify family myths with regard to gender issues

Measurements:

1. Client verbal report
2. Therapist Discharge Summary

Objective: To assist the family through the court process

Measurements:

1. Therapist notes completed after each treatment session
2. Therapist Discharge Summary
3. Client verbal report

STAFFING

The program employs two full-timc social workcrs, a half-timc psychologist and one half-time secretary. The half-time Program Director is provided by the Social Work Department, Rockyview General Hospital. A volunteer works with the program one day per week. Consultation from a pediatrician, and a psychiatrist are available in the program.

The FSATP draws upon an interdisciplinary advisory group presently established within Children and Family Services. It consists of representatives from nursing, pediatrics, psychiatry, psychology and emergency services at the hospital.

CONCLUSION

The FSATP has been in operation for four years. It continues to modify both assessment and treatment processes based on feedback from clients, professionals and the beginning evaluation of service. Over the next 18 months the list of objectives and activities will be expanded in order to incorporate changes introduced in the past two years. These changes will more accurately reflect the current objectives of the FSATP as well as the complex nature of cases of child sexual abuse. Ongoing feedback from clients, professionals and evaluation will continue to influence the ongoing development and operation of the program.

Appendix 1
Measurement Tools

1.	Minnesota Multiphasic Personality Inventory	14 years and up	All age-appropriate family members
2.	Faces III a) Describing family as it is now b) Describing family as you would like it to be	12 years and up	All age-appropriate family members
3.	Personality Inventory for Children (P.I.C.)	Children 6-16	Mother/Father/Perpetrator each rate the children in the family
4.	Parent/Adolescent Communication (Parent Form)	Parents/Marital Dyad	Mother/Father each rate all family members 12–18 years of age
5.	Parent/Adolescent Communication (Adolescent Form) a) rating Mother b) rating Father	12 years and up	All family members rate Mother/Father
6.	Coopersmith Self-Esteem Scales a) school form b) adult form	8–15; 16 years and up	All age-appropriate family members
7.	Children's Personality Questionnaire (C.P.Q.)	8–11 years	All age-appropriate family members
8.	High School Personality Questionnaire (H.S.P.Q.)	12–13 years	All age-appropriate family members
9.	Child Anxiety Scale (C.A.S.)	5–12 years	All age-appropriate family members
10.	Children's Depression Inventory	1–13 years	All age-appropriate family members
11.	Family Environment Scale (F.E.S.) (Form R)	12 years and up	All age-appropriate family members
12.	Index of Marital Satisfaction (M.I.S.)	Parents/Marital Dyad	Parents/Marital Dyad
13.	Index of Sexual Satisfaction (I.S.S.)	Parents/Marital Dyad	Parents/Marital Dyad
14.	Sexual Meaning Scale	Parents/Marital Dyad	Parents/Marital Dyad
15.	File: Family Inventory of Life Events and Changes		Administered to family by Therapist — completed by Therapist
16.	A-File: Adolescent-Family Inventory of Life Events and Changes	12–18 years	Administered to Adolescents by Therapist — completed by Therapist
17.	Olson-Clinical Rating Scale		Subjective Rating of Family by Therapist

NOTES

1. At the time of writing Ms. Babins-Wagner was the Director of the Family Sexual Abuse Treatment Program, Department of Social Work, Rockyview General Hospital, Calgary, Alberta.

ACKNOWLEDGEMENT

For permission to reproduce Tables 1 and 2 the author wishes to acknowledge Larson, N., and Maddock, J. (1986). Structural and functional variables in incest family systems: Implications for assessment and treatment. In T. Trepper and M.J. Barrett (Eds.), *Treating incest: A multimodal systems perspective* (pp. 27–44). The Haworth Press, Inc., 10 Alice Street, Binghamton, NY, 13904.

REFERENCES

Alexander, P.C. (1985). A systems theory conceptualization of incest. *Family Process, 24*(1), 79–88.

Anderson, C., & Stewart, C. (1983). *Mastering resistance.* New York: Guilford.

Andolfi, M., Angelo, C., Menghi, P., & Nicolo-Corigliano, A.M.C. (1983). *Behind the family mask.* New York: Brunner/Mazel.

Aponte, H.J., & VanDeusen, J.M. (1981). Structural family therapy. In A.S. Gurman & D.P. Knishkern (Eds.), *Handbook of family therapy* (pp. 310–360). New York: Brunner/Mazel.

Authier, K. (1983). Incest and sexual violence. In J.C. Hansen (Ed.), *Sexual issues in family therapy* (Family Therapy Collection) (pp. 101–127). Maryland: Aspen System Corp.

Babins-Wagner, R., & Miller, C. (1985). *Child abuse and family systems approach to therapy: The development of a model.* Unpublished paper.

Bagley, C. (1985). *Child sexual abuse within the family: An account of studies 1978–1984.* (Monograph Series No. 18). The University of Calgary, Faculty of Social Welfare.

Barlow, D.H., Hayes, S., & Nelson, R.D. (1984). *The scientist practitioner* (p. 163). New York: Pergamon Press.

Barrett, M.J., Sykes, C., & Byrnes, W. (1986). A systemic model for the treatment of intrafamilial child sexual abuse. In T. Trepper & M.J. Barrett (Eds.), *Treating incest: A multimodal systems perspective* (pp. 67–82). Binghamton, NY: Haworth Press.

Barton, C., & Alexander, J.F. (1981). Functional family therapy. In A.S. Gurman & D.P. Knishkern (Eds.), *Handbook of Family Therapy*. New York: Brunner/Mazel.

Beavers, W.R. (1985). *Successful marriage: A family systems approach to couples therapy*. New York: Norton & Co.

Benjamin, A. (1969). *The helping interview* (2nd Ed.). Boston: Houghton Mifflin Co.

Bergman, J. (1985). *Fishing for barracuda*. New York: Norton & Co.

Boscolo, L., Gecchin, G., Hoffman, L., & Penn, P. (1987). *Milan systemic family therapy*. New York: Basic Books.

Bowen, M. (1966). The use of family theory in clinical practice. In M. Bowen (Ed.), *Family therapy in clinical practice* (pp. 147–182). New York: Jason Aronson.

Cade, B. (1987). Brief/strategic approaches to therapy. *Australia and New Zealand Journal of Family Therapy, 8*(1), 37–44.

Carter, E.A., & McGoldrick, M. (1980). *The family life cycle*. New York: Gardner Press.

Cohen, T. (1983). The incestuous family revisited. *Social Casework: The Journal of Contemporary Social Work, 64*(3), 154–161.

Cole, C. (1983). Sexual disorders and the family therapist. In J.C. Hansen (Ed.), *Sexual issues in family therapy* (pp. 49–61). Family Therapy Collection. Maryland: Aspen System Corp.

Corcoran, R., & Fisher, J. (1987). *Measures for clinical practice, a source book*. New York: Free Press.

De Schazer, S. (1982a). *Brief family therapy*. New York: Guilford Press.

De Schazer, S. (1982b). Problem centered systems therapy of the family. In A.S. Gurman, & D.P. Knishkern (Eds.), *Handbook of family therapy* (pp. 444–482). New York: Brunner/Mazel.

Efron, D. (1986). *Journeys: Expansion of the strategic-systemic therapies*. New York: Brunner/Mazel.

Epstein, N., & Bishop, D. (1981). Problem centered systems therapy of the family. In A.S. Gurman & D.P. Knishkern (Eds.), *Handbook of family therapy* (pp. 444–482). New York: Brunner/Mazel.

Finkelhor, D. (1986). *A sourcebook on child sexual abuse*. Beverly Hills, CA: Sage.

Finkelhor, D. (1984). *Child sexual abuse: New theory and research*. New York: The Free Press.

Finkelhor, D. (1979). *Sexually victimized children*. New York: The Free Press.

Fisch, R., Weakland, J.H., & Segal, L. (1982). *The tactics of change*. San Francisco: Jossey-Bass.

Fredman, N., & Sherman, R. (1987). *Handbook of measurements for marriage and family therapy*. New York: Brunner/Mazel.

Freeman, D. (1980). *Perspectives on family therapy.* Vancouver: Butterworth & Co.

Garbarino, J., Guttman, E., & Seeley, J.W. (1986). *The psychologically battered child.* San Francisco, CA: Jossey-Bass.

Giarretto, H. (1982). *Treatment of sexual abuse: A treatment training model.* Palo Alto, CA: Sciences and Behavior Books.

Giarretto, H. (1978). Humanistic treatment of father daughter incest. *Journal of Humanistic Psychology, 18,* 17–21.

Goodrich, T.J., Rampage, C., Ellsman, B., & Halstead, K. (1988), *Feminist family.* New York: Norton & Co.

Groth, A.N., Hobson, W.F., & Gray, T.S. (1982). The child molester: Clinical observations. *Journal of Social Work and Human Sexuality, 1,* 129–44.

Gurman, A.S. (1985). *Casebook of marital therapy.* New York: Guilford Press.

Haley, J. (1980). *Leaving home.* New York: McGraw-Hill.

Haley, J. (1976). *Problem solving therapy: New strategies for effective family therapy.* New York: Harper & Row.

Haley, J. (1967). Toward a theory of pathological systems. In G. Zuk & I. Boszormenyi-Nagy (Eds.), *Family therapy and disturbed families* (pp. 11–27). Palo Alto, CA: Science and Behavior Books.

Haley, J. (1984). *Ordeal therapy.* San Francisco, CA: Jossey-Bass.

Haley, J., & Hoffman, L. (1967). *Techniques of family therapy.* San Francisco, CA: Basic Books.

Hartman, A., & Laird, J. (1983). *Family centred social work practice.* New York: Free Press.

Heiman, J.R., Gladue, B.A., Roberts, C.S., & Lopiccolo, J. (1986). Historical and current factors discriminating sexually functional from sexually dysfunctional married couples. *Journal of Marital and Family Therapy, 12*(2), 163–174.

Hoffman, L. (1981). *Foundation of family therapy.* New York: Basic Books.

Hornick, J.P., Kerr, N., & Raiken, S. (1987). A model for short-term process/cost analysis within the context of a long-term evaluation of family support programs. *The Canadian Journal of Program Evaluation, 2*(2), 37–49.

Jacobson, N.S., & Gurman, A.S. (Eds.). (1968). *Clinical handbook of marital therapy.* New York: Guilford Press.

James, B., & Nasjleti, M. (1983). *Treating sexually abused children and their families.* Palo Alto, CA: Consulting Psychologists Press.

Justice, B., & Justice, R. (1979). *The broken taboo: Sex in the family.* New York: Human Sciences Press.

Kantor, D., & Lehr, W. (1977). *Inside the family.* San Francisco, CA: Jossey-Bass.

Keeney, B. (1983). *Aesthetics of change.* New York: Guilford Press.

Kempe, H.C., & Kemp, R.S. (1984). *The common secret: Sexual abuse of children and adolescents.* New York: W.H. Freeman & Co.

Kennedy, M., & Cormier, B.M. (1969). Father-daughter incest: Treatment of the family. *Laval Medical, 40,* 946–950.

Kerr, M.E. (1981). Family systems theory and therapy. In A.S. Gurman & D.P. Knishkern (Eds.), *Handbook of family therapy* (pp. 110–120). New York: Brunner/Mazel.

Kroth, J.A. (1979). *Child sexual abuse: Analysis of a family therapy approach.* Springfield, IL: Charles C. Thomas.

Larson, N.R. (1980). *An analysis of the effectiveness of a state-sponsored program designed to teach intervention skills in the treatment of family sexual abuse.* Unpublished doctoral dissertation, University of Minnesota, Minneapolis, MN.

Larson, N.R., & Maddock, J.W. (1983). Incest and other sexual contacts between adults and children. In C.C. Nadelson & D.B. Marcotte (Eds.), *Treatment intervention in human sexuality* (pp. 157–179). New York: Plenum Press.

Larson, N., & Maddock, J. (1986). Structural and functional variables in incest family systems: Implications for assessment and treatment. In T. Trepper & M.J. Barrett (Eds.), *Treating incest: A multimodal systems perspective* (pp. 27–44). Binghamton, NY: Haworth Press.

Leahey, M., & Wright, L. (Eds.). *Families and psychosocial problems* (pp. 179–194). Springhouse, PA: Springhouse Corporation.

Lustig, N., Dresser, J.W., Spellman, S.W., & Murray, T.B. (1966). Incest: A family group survival pattern. In *Archives of general psychiatry, 14,* 31-40.

MacFarlane, K., Waterman, J., Conerly, S., Damon, L., Durfee, M., & Long, S. (Eds.). (1986). *Sexual abuse of young children.* New York: Guilford Press.

MacKinnon, L.K., & James, K. (1987). The Milan systemic approach: Theory and practice. *Australia and New Zealand Journal of Family Therapy, 8*(2), 37–44.

Madanes, C. (1981). *Strategic family therapy.* San Francisco, CA: Jossey-Bass.

Madanes, C. (1984). *Behind the one-way mirror: Advances in the practice of strategic therapy.* San Francisco, CA: Jossey-Bass.

Maddock, J. (1983). Human sexuality in the life cycle of the family system. In J.C. Hansen (Ed.), *Sexual issues in family therapy* (pp. 1–31). Family Therapy Collections. Maryland: Aspen System Corp.

Maish, H. (1972). *Incest.* (C.Bearne, Trans.). New York: Slein & Day.

Meiselman, K. (1981). *Incest: A psychological study of causes and effects with treatment recommendations* (3rd Ed.). San Francisco, CA: Jossey-Bass.

Miller, V., & Mansfield, E. (1981). Family therapy for the multiple incest family. *Journal of Psychiatric Nursing and Mental Health Services, 19*(4), 29–32.

Minuchin, S. (1974). *Families and family therapy.* Cambridge, MA: Harvard University Press.

Minuchin, S., & Fishman, H.C. (1979). *Family therapy techniques.* Cambridge, MA: Harvard University Press.

Morris, L.L., & Fitz-Gibbon, C.T. (1978). *Evaluator's handbook.* Beverly Hills, CA: Sage.

Mrazek, P.B., & Bentovim, A. (1981). Incest and the dysfunctional family system. In P.B. Mrazek & C.H. Kempe (Eds.), *Sexually abused children and their families* (pp. 167–178). Oxford: Pergamon.

Nelson, S.T., Fleuridas, C., & Rosenthal, D. (1986). The evolution of circular questions: Training family therapists. *Journal of marital and family therapy, 12*(2), 113–127.

O'Brien, M., & Bera, W. (1986). Adolescent sexual offenders: A descriptive typology. *Preventing sexual abuse, 1*(3), 1–4.

Palazzoli, M.S., Boscolo, L., Cecchin, G., & Prata, G. (1981). *Paradox and counter paradox.* New York: Jason Aronson.

Papp, P. (1983). *The process of change.* New York: Guilford Press.

Pelletier, G., & Handy, L.C. (1986). Family dysfunction and the psychological impact of child sexual abuse. *Canadian Journal of Psychiatry, 31*, 407–411.

Penn, P. (1982). Multigenerational issues in strategic therapy of sexual problems. *Journal of Strategic and Systemic Therapies, 1*(3), 1–13.

Reimer, S. (1940). A research note on incest. *American Journal of Sociology, 45*, 556–575.

Reposa, R.E., & Zuelzer, M.B. (1983). Family therapy with incest. *International Journal of Family Therapy, 5*(2), 111–126.

Roberts, J. (1986). An evolving model: Links between the Milan approach and strategic models of family therapy. In D.E. Efron (Ed.), *Journeys: Expansion of the strategic-systemic therapies* (pp. 150–173). New York: Brunner/Mazel.

Rossi, P.H., & Freeman, H.E. (1986). *Evaluation: A systemic approach* (pp. 147, 150–155). Beverly Hills, CA: Sage.

Russell, D.H. (1986). *The secret trauma: Incest in the lives of girls and women.* New York: Basic Books.

Sever, J.C., & Janzen, C. (1982). Reconstitution of sexually abusive families. *Child Welfare, 61*(5), 286.

Sgroi, S.M. (1982). *Handbook of clinical intervention in child sexual abuse* (pp. 241–267). Lexington, MA: Lexington Press.

Skepple, I.V. (1984). Coping strategies of the violent family: The case of incest. *Psychiatric Nursing, 11/12.*

Stanton, D. (1981). Strategic. In A.S. Gurman & D.P. Knishkern (Eds.), *Handbook of family therapy* (pp. 351–402). New York: Brunner/Mazel.
Straus, M.A. (1973). A general systems theory approach to a theory of violence between family members. *Social Science Information, 12,* 105–125.
Straus, M.A. (1986). Stress and child abuse. In C.H. Kempe & R.E. Helfer (Eds.), *The battered child* (3rd Ed., pp. 86–103). Chicago: University of Chicago Press.
Swan, R.W. (1985). The child as active participant in sexual abuse. *Clinical Social Work Journal, 13*(1), 62–77.
Taylor, R.L. (1984). Marital therapy in the treatment of incest. *Social Casework: The Journal of Contemporary Social Work, 65*(4), 195–202.
Thorman, G. (1983). *Incestuous families.* Springfield, IL: Charles C. Thomas.
Trepper, T.S., & Barrett, M.J. (1986). Vulnerability to incest: A framework for assessment. *Treating incest: A multimodal systems perspective* (pp. 13–14). Binghamton, NY: Haworth Press.
Trepper, T.S., & Barrett, M.J. (1989). *Systemic treatment of incest.* New York: Brunner/Mazel.
Trepper, T.S., & Traicoff, E. (1983). Treatment of intrafamily sexuality: Issues in therapy and research. *Journal of Sex Education and Therapy, 9*(1), 14–18.
Watzlawick, P., Weakland, J., & Fisch, R. (1974). *Change.* New York: Norton & Co.
Weinburg, S.K. (1955). *Incest behaviour.* New York: Citadel.

Journal of Child and Youth Care Special Issue Pages 129 – 139
 ISSN 0840-982X

Child Care Commentary
We Get a Life Sentence: Young People in Care Speak Out on Child Sexual Abuse

Brian Raychaba

BACKGROUND

This report offers the views and opinions of young people in child welfare care on the issue of child sexual abuse in Canada and is predicated on the assumption that consumer feedback and involvement of young people in evaluation of programs enhances the quality of services offered. It was prepared by a member of the national Youth in Care Network with the input of a number of young people and presented at the "*Reaching for Solutions*" National Strategy Workshop on Child Sexual Abuse organized by the Special Advisor to the Minister of Child Sexual Abuse in September 1989.

The Fifth Annual Meeting of the National Youth in Care Network (NYICN) was held 18–23 May 1989 in Calgary, Alberta, Canada. Thirty-six young people in/from the care of child welfare authorities attended, representing every province as well as the Yukon Territories. The group was informed that a national consultation on the sexual abuse of children was being held and that our National Development Officer, a 20-year-old former ward, would be attending on behalf of the YNICN. The young people expressed their desire and willingness to offer some feedback based on their collective experience of sexual abuse and/or family violence. One of the youth present prepared a questionnaire which all the attending youth were asked to fill out. This was done as a means of providing the consultation participants with some additional information. The questionnaire and responses are included at the end of this report. Of the thirty-two young people who responded to the questionnaire, six males and fifteen females reported having been victimized sexually by parents, strangers, or caregivers within the child welfare system.

A smaller number within the larger group agreed to meet one evening and focus discussion specifically on the issue of child sexual abuse. Most of those involved in this smaller discussion group were survivors, both male and female, of child sexual abuse. A few, however, while not the victims of child sexual abuse nonetheless asked to take part. The group agreed to let them sit in. The young people decided to focus on a number of specific areas of concern: legal issues; rural/remote areas and Native communities; treatment issues; public awareness and primary prevention. The remainder of this report relates *their* views and perspectives on a subject of which they have firsthand experience and knowledge.

LEGAL ISSUES

Child sexual abuse is one of the most serious and damaging of criminal offences. We, the victims, are violated and hurt in a most private manner. Why does sentencing for convicted perpetrators not reflect this reality? One young woman in our group said that the individual who molested her received a one-year suspended sentence. Is child sexual abuse a crime or isn't it? We question whether the legal system at this point in time really believes that it is. We receive a "life sentence" regardless of what happens to the offender. A maximum three-year suspended sentence is unjustifiable in our opinion. If child sexual abuse is to be perceived and addressed as a serious social problem, the legal system must take the first step in the form of stronger sentencing.

We, the victims, should not have to decide whether or not we want a parent or family member charged in cases of intrafamilial abuse. This places undue stress and responsibility on us. It leads to further self-blame and is an additional form of victimization. We feel bad enough as it is.

If and when we refuse to testify in court, this is due to fear, threats from perpetrators, and/or a general sense of being overpowered by circumstances beyond our control. Child victims should never, under any instance, be prosecuted for contempt of court if they refuse to testify. We are the most innocent party in that courtroom. We should not be punished for being afraid or uncertain.

Many in our group questioned whether all persons present in the courtroom during their testimony really had to be there. Are they all really necessary? We would prefer a more personable, private and "safe" environment (i.e., a judge's chambers).

We believe wholeheartedly that videotaping and closed-circuit televisions are invaluable in the court setting. These resources make it much easier for a child victim to testify. Children/young people are easily intimidated and may "clamp up" in court. We need a safe and secure environment.

We believe that in most jurisdictions insufficient attention is paid to the special vulnerabilities of being a child witness. Survivors in our group spoke of how they were "raked over the coals" in court by defending attorneys. One told of how her past personal history (in particular her sexual activity) was brought up in court in an attempt to discredit her case. Child sexual abuse, like adult rape, is not a sexual crime but a crime of violence. We strongly recommend that responsible officials within the Canadian legal system see to it that a code of ethics for attorney cross-examining child witnesses be developed and instituted.

Related to this is the issue of training and education. Legal practitioners such as judges and lawyers need to have adequate knowledge of the dynamics of child sexual abuse as well as an understanding of the special needs, vulnerabilities, and limited capacities of child witnesses. Defence attorneys must be trained in more non-damaging forms of cross examination.

Delaying therapy treatment until completion of court proceedings is wrong and unacceptable. This serves the system more than it does the victim. We need skilled help, someone we can talk to who knows where we are coming from, as soon as possible.

We believe very strongly that out-of-court disclosure statements should be deemed admissible in court. Repeated disclosure, especially in the semi-public courtroom setting is unnecessary, and it hurts to talk about it.

We believe very strongly that in cases of incest or intrafamilial molestation it should be the *accused* and *not* the *victim* who is forced to leave the home pending trial. Placing us in child welfare care tells us that *we* have done something wrong and that *we* are being punished. We have committed no crime. Concern over the individual liberty and "property rights" of the accused is not a valid reason for depriving us of our right to a real family.

On behalf of future child victims, we ask that friendly and "neutral" child support personnel be made available throughout the entire court process, to hold our hand or just simply be there.

Individuals in our group spoke of having to wait months and even years for their cases to come to court. We have friends who actually dropped their cases due to family pressures, general stress, and the long wait. We would ask that the legal system make every effort to give child sexual abuse cases priority with respect to scheduling. The time between disclosure and trial is fraught with stress, anxiety, and uncertainty and should be made as brief as possible. Until legal issues are resolved, we cannot fully start our lives over again and carry on.

What about treatment for the perpetrator? This is especially crucial in cases of intrafamilial abuse. A number of young people in the group told of how they had been pushed by social workers and others to prosecute; then, after the trial, both the legal and child welfare systems failed to follow through and ensure that offenders received treatment. One young woman said that when the perpetrator in her case failed to continue treatment the courts did nothing to correct this. The lack of mandatory treatment for sex offenders again raises the question of whether or not society truly believes that molesting a child is a crime. We receive treatment while in care but offenders usually do not. This tells us that there is something wrong with *us*, that *we*, and *only we*, are in need of "repair" or "fixing." Overall, we feel the entire court system does not validate either *us* or our claims. As a lack of physical evidence is common place, the cards are usually stacked against us.

We feel that using the civil courts to sue perpetrators for compensation is a valid option which should be explored further. Victims should have at their disposal a number of options and alternatives. We support proposals to amend existing legislation so that adult survivors, of whatever age, can commence suits against offenders. Expiration of the statutory limitation period is an unnecessary impediment to justice. Due to the very real scars inflicted and the time that it takes for healing to occur, it may be years until we are capable of testifying in court.

We are very concerned with the rate of abuse in foster and institutional child welfare care. Present screening and complaints procedures are inadequate. Of the 21 previously sexually abused young people attending the Calgary meeting, 11 had been sexually abused *while in care*. In one person's case, her first sexually abusive experience occurred only *after* she had come into care. Perpetrators ranged from foster parents and child care workers to foster siblings and others. We would strongly support moves to allow child- and youth-serving agencies access to the criminal records of applicants whether child care workers, social workers, foster parents, or other individuals responsible for children and young people, with the applicant's consent. If he or she refuses consent, then it should be lawful for the particular agency to refuse them employment. It is important that all provinces and territories have in place pro-active, flexible, and "user friendly" child/youth in care complaints procedures.

We are saddened by the public backlash against screening mechanisms such as the Child Abuse Registry in Ontario. The majority of sexual abuse cases do not make it to court because of either lack of evidence or the victim's unwillingness to lay charges. Sexual abuse has still happened; there is a victim and there is an offender. What about the other children at home, our brothers, sisters, nieces, and nephews? We are in care but what about them? And what about the children in our neighborhood, in our community? Does not their welfare and well-being merit the most stringent precautions on society's part? The individual right of the perpetrator to privacy infringes upon children's collective right to protection. Whose "rights" will prevail? Society must decide.

TREATMENT ISSUES

Safety is crucial in treatment for victims of child sexual abuse. Although treatment is based on the safety, protection, and well-being of those being treated, we question whether this is, in fact, happening. One young person in our group spoke of a residential treatment situation in which adolescent victims and offenders were placed *together* in one treatment home due to a lack of resources. Sexual assaults on previously victimized young women took place frequently despite the best efforts of an overworked staff. This is not an atmosphere conducive to healing. The lack of specialized treatment resources must be addressed. If it is not, then the treatment process, which is intended to promote healing, may likely become yet another form of victimization.

Another young woman spoke of how, upon entering the care system, it was she and not her abuser who became the focus of treatment. "I was the problem, not the abuse. All of the sudden I had all of these personal problems I never knew about before." In her opinion, treatment itself came to constitute an additional form of victimization.

None of us in the group had access to any form of self-help group as an option when we first came into care. We all agreed that talking with peers who had similar experiences and who came from similar circumstance would have furthered our personal healing process. Participation in youth-in-care groups provides those who have not yet disclosed with a "safe" environment where they can talk about and begin to deal with issues related to being a sexual abuse victim. The focus of these groups is on being in care rather than on having been sexually abused; this 'less risky' focus is seen as beneficial. A number in the group disclosed for the first time at our meeting.

It is vitally important that those treating us recognize that we must be party to our own healing. The treatment system at the present time, we feel, is not child or young person focused. One individual said that at the time she needed some sense of control and power over her own life, a say regarding who she would see, who she would talk to. Choice is crucial. We know what helps us and what does not. We must have a say in the design, implementation, and evaluation of particular treatment programs. Timing is also important; children and young people need "their time" and do not appreciate being "pushed" into treatment too far and too fast. We demand that child victims be allowed to simply be children. Do not force us to grow up too quickly. Allow us time to be just children. Forcing us to "deal with the issues" at such an early age constitutes a theft of our childhood.

One component lacking in the treatment programs of survivors in our group was some orientation and awareness in matters of basic human sexuality, relationships, and sexual identity. This was the case particularly with survivors in our group (both male and female) who had been victimized by members of the same sex and who now find themselves confronted with particular issues relating to sexual identity.

We all agreed that what did or would have helped was a relationship with someone we could trust who had some experience with or knowledge of the issues involved. Self-help groups and voluntary programs such as Big Sisters/Big Brothers, where issues and problems can be discussed in confidence, were put forward as ways of meeting our need for this particular type of "treatment."

We need a continuum of treatment/care with intensive one-on-one support from disclosure through court proceedings, treatment, and after-care follow-up. In a sense, treatment should never end since the abuse is never forgotten. All treatment programs, whether linked with a child welfare organization or independent, should include an after-care drop-in component, some place where survivors can return and talk to someone if and when issues emerge or re-emerge.

Identification and treatment of young sex offenders is crucial. One young person reported of having been molested by a foster sibling while another admitted to having been abuser.

RURAL, REMOTE, AND NATIVE COMMUNITIES

It is imperative in Native communities that concerned local people be supported, trained, and empowered to confront the issue in their own areas. Outsiders simply do not understand the unique inner workings of this problem within these communities. Only one of the young people in our group was of Native background, however, her comments proved extremely insightful. She spoke of having been assaulted during a visit to a Reserve and noted that at the time she was not even aware that her attack was wrong. "I thought he was just a bad boy. I didn't know it wasn't right." Awareness and preventative education for Native and other children in rural and remote areas is very necessary.

The group agreed that more trained professionals are needed in remote areas. An economic incentive program was suggested as one way to entice much-needed professionals to these regions. Many rural areas exhibit a very slack hush-hush attitude towards child abuse. As one young person puts it, "You hear so much, but so little gets done." One possible way of rectifying the dilemma faced by victimized children and young people living in complacent social settings would be the introduction of no-questions-asked "safe houses" which would at least provide abused youth with somewhere to go. A greater supply of resources of all kinds is needed in outlying areas.

Another young person, who was of West Indian background, chose to define the word 'remote' in terms of being from a different and alien culture. She explained how in West Indian culture child sexual abuse and incest are kept very much a family secret. With the stresses resulting from immigration along with culture shock, immigrant families often become isolated and as a result often close in on themselves. "I think sometimes they just do not know or acknowledge the fact that they are in a new culture." She believed that social workers from her specific ethnic group (i.e., West Indian) would have probably done more for her and her family than uninformed outsiders.

PRIMARY PREVENTION AND PUBLIC AWARENESS

We feel that preventive education in schools is crucial and that programs such as the "Safe and Happy Personal Safety Kit" are essential. Perpetrators often tell child victims that what is happening is a "good thing." Children need a healthy standard of behaviour and conduct with which to compare with that of the offender. Sex education in schools is also essential. It must begin in the earlier grades. The sooner the better.

Availability of parenting education/training must be broadened through the auspices of continuing education, public health, extended post-natal classes, church groups, etc. There is also a role for the private sector/business community. Many companies already offer courses aimed at helping employees quit smoking, lose weight, etc. Why not provide child care courses for those employees with children?

Many of the young people in the group expressed their fear of becoming abusive parents themselves. We often catch ourselves displaying the same behaviour as abusive parents, acting towards children like our parents acted towards us. We need to learn what is normal in family relationships. Child welfare agencies must offer extensive after-care services for youth formerly in their care, including counselling, drug and alcohol rehabilitation services, and (for those with children who are willing to attend) parent education courses stressing coping skills and non-physical forms of child management. Steps must be taken to heal the hurt and stop detrimental individual and family dynamics in order to break the cycle of abuse.

As mentioned earlier, a number of youth noted the benefits of tutors/ Big Brothers/Big Sisters types of organizations. Others in the group commented that an adult friend — someone we could talk to, someone apart from the family — would have been much appreciated.

Some victimized children/young people are prone to becoming sex offenders themselves. One young woman attending the wider meeting admitted to having sexually abused another young person while in care. Treatment of the adolescent sex offender must be given top priority if only to reduce the multiple victims they produce as they grow up. Efforts must be made to identify and treat them early.

Issues relating to family violence and the empowerment of women and single mothers also emerged. Many of us related family histories in which characteristically poor, isolated, and depressed single mothers came to find themselves in exploitative relationships with violent and often abusive men. Stepfathers and violent boyfriends are, as we heard from many of the group members, among those most likely to offend or abuse sexually. In their personal struggles to cope with distressing circumstances, our mothers felt incredibly unempowered and not in control of their own lives. As a result, we reason that they looked for love, stability, security, and some sense of control over their lives in relationships with these men. These relationships, however, all too often turned out to be exploitative and violent.

Child welfare agencies often enter the home and criticize what they see. But where is the support to help make change possible? One young person stated that, in his case, weekly if not daily visits and one-on-one support work would have been necessary to reduce the potential for family violence at home.

General public awareness was highlighted by the group as very important. Children and young people must be allowed an awareness, an understanding of sexual abuse as the crime that it is. Many of the young survivors in our group spoke of having felt alone and different, as if sexual abuse was something that had happened only to them. Some were frightened of disclosing because they felt no one would believe them. Others said that, at the time, they simply did not realize that the abuse was wrong. All agreed that greater media-oriented public awareness campaigns are necessary to promote a more reality-oriented and accepting climate of public opinion, an environment in which children will be empowered to speak out if and when they are being mistreated. The realization that others have suffered similar experiences and that they will understand is itself the first step towards healing. Fear of an increased need of child welfare services due to a greater number of disclosures is not a justifiable reason for failing to make people aware of what is happening, and for neglecting to tell victims that they are not alone.

The time for a multi-mass media based public awareness campaign is *now*. This is timely and very necessary. Such a campaign should focus on both the *extent* and *nature* of the problem. We feel that niceties should be put aside and a more specific, perhaps blunt, message conveyed. The focus should be on the reality of this phenomenon (i.e., "Child sexual abuse is happening in our community"). A "soft" approach built around local initiatives and success stories would be ineffective in our opinion. We, as Canadians, have to admit *ownership* of child sexual abuse; otherwise, it simply remains a terrible crime committed by *other* people. The focus must be on *us*, not *them*, and should stress the lifelong scars left on the victims. "*We get a life sentence.*" If we truly wish to act seriously on this very serious social problem, any public awareness campaign will have to employ a "hard" approach.

DISCUSSION AND CONCLUSION

This report has attempted to demonstrate that when empowered to speak and address topics such as child sexual abuse on their own behalf, young people in child welfare care are capable of providing professional caregivers and policy architects crucial insights into issues and realities uniquely their own. In addition, it also raises questions for academics in the field regarding research methodologies. Commenting on the preceding report and its findings on sexual abuse in child welfare care, American researcher Emily Jean McFadden (1989) recently stated the following:

> I will admit it is a small sample, and probably did not follow a rigorous methodology. However, it is in violent contrast to U.S. research, a juxtaposition of incongruent opposites, when compared with many well-known studies. Fansel and Shinn (1978), Jones and Moses (1984), Maluccio and Fein (1985) and Festinger (1983) have never unearthed such horrifying data, as that which Brian found with his self-help methodology.
>
> Could it be that the young people lied to Brian? I doubt it. Could it be that Canadians are more sexually abusive than citizens of the U.S.? I doubt it.
>
> Or could there be a remote possibility that American researchers have been asking the wrong questions? Could it be that youth in care are more likely to open up to Brian Raychaba than to a professor? What are we to conclude about all those studies which show that children do fairly well in foster care? If there are researchers in this room, I challenge you to think of ways in which we can generate the same candor in youth as groups like the National Association of Young People in Care Great Britain, and the National Youth in Care Network. Any study of children in care should have a youth advisory board, and perhaps use youth as interviewers.

"It is time to listen carefully," she concluded, "and then allow young people to move ahead to the goal of empowerment."

As with the relationship between young people in care and adult caregivers, so too must the relationship between youth in care and child welfare researchers change from one in which the former are studied by the latter at a distance as objects to one in which both participate in research endeavours together as subjects. It has been shown that empowering young people in care to speak on their own behalf results in tremendous personal benefits and growth for those involved. An added windfall for caregivers and child welfare researchers may well be a more accurate view of life in care as experienced by young people.

REFERENCES

McFadden, E.J. (1989, August). *Impowering children and youth foster care*. Paper presented at the International Foster Care 6th Annual Conference, Eastern Michigan University, Ypslanti, MI.

SEXUAL ABUSE QUESTIONNAIRE

1. What sex are you?

Male:	13
Female:	19

2. Have you been sexually abused?

	Male	Female
Yes:	6	15
No:	7	4

3. If **Yes**, how many offenders?

No.	Male	Female
one	3	5
two	1	5
three	2	0
four	0	1
seven	0	1
"lots"	0	2
no ans.	0	1

4. Were you abused by:

	Male	Female	Both
Male Respondents:	1	2	3
Female Respondents	12	0	3

5. Were you abused by:

	Male	Female
Relative	2	9
Friend	3	4
Babysitter	1	0
Stranger	2	3
Other	2	10

6. Were you abused in Care?

	Male	Female
Yes	3	8
No	3	7

7. Were you abused by:

	Male	Female
Social Worker	0	0
Child Care Worker	2	2
Foster Parent	0	6
Other	1	0
Foster brother	0	2

8. Who did you open up to?

	Male	Female
Friend	2	7
Worker	2	5
Relative	1	0
Parents	1	1
Teacher	0	2
No One	2	0

9. Did you blame yourself:

	Male	Female
Yes	4	10
No	2	5

10. What kind of help did you get?

	Male	Female
Friends	0	1
Foster Parents	0	1
Workers	0	1
Counselling	0	5
Psychiatrist	1	0
None	5	7

11. Did the person you told believe you?

	Male	Female
Yes	4	9
No	1	4
Not believed at first	1	1
No answer	1	1

12. Did the help you received get you over blaming yourself? Was it helpful?

	Male	Female
Yes	4	6
No	0	2
Sort of	1	2
No answer	0	5

13. Do you still feel it was your fault?

	Male	Female
Yes	1	3
No	4	7
"Half and half"	1	2
No answer	0	3

14. How do you feel about yourself now?

	Male	Female
Mixed	1	4
Fine	3	9
No answer	2	2

15. Did you say no or try to say no?

	Male	Female
Yes	1	8
No	4	5
No answer	1	2

Journal of Child and Youth Care Special Issue Pages 141 – 152

Review Article
Advancing Knowledge on Child Sexual Abuse, and the Prosecution and Treatment of Offenders

There is a knowledge explosion in the field of child sexual abuse, and it is vitally important for child and youth care workers to try and keep abreast of the many important clinical and research studies which appear in journals, books and monographs almost daily. In previous reviews in this journal (Bagley, 1982, 1983) we have summarized journal and monograph publications, and more recently have published extensive reviews of available literature since 1982 (Bagley & Thurston, 1989; Bagley & Thomlison, 1991). The present review article is an extension of this work. Hopefully, many more review articles will appear, helping practitioners keep abreast of this important knowledge explosion!

Of particular interest is the increase in studies of offenders and offender therapy. It is now clear that the motivation to offend sexually begins in adolescence or earlier, and that key interventions by therapists and child and youth care workers through these early "windows of opportunity" can be very cost effective in a number of cases.

REFERENCES

Bagley, C. (1982). Childhood sexuality and the sexual abuse of children: A review of monograph literature 1978 to 1982. *Journal of Child and Youth Care, 1*(3), 105–127.

Bagley, C. (1983). Child sexual abuse: Annotated bibliography of journal studies 1988–1982. *Journal of Child and Youth Care, 1*(5), 81–86.

Bagley, C., & Thurston, W. (1989). Preventing child sexual abuse: Key research. *Rehabilitation and Health Monographs, 18*, 1–369.

Bagley, C., & Thomlison, R. (1991). *Child sexual abuse: Prevention and treatment.* Toronto: Wall and Emerson.

❧ ❧ ❧

Karin Meiselman. *Resolving the Trauma of Incest.* San Francisco, CA: Jossey-Bass, 320 pp.

Meiselman's first book on incest, its nature and its therapy was published in 1978. For this reviewer, the book was a revelation and set in train a process of intellectual reformulation which led to a program of research and the development of new therapeutic systems for helping former victims of child sexual abuse (Bagley & King, 1990).

It is clear that although as many as 30 percent of women (and about half that proportion in men) will have experienced unwanted sexual contact in childhood, a much smaller proportion will have experienced incestuous abuse, according to the various definitions offered by researchers. In its most restricted, legal definition, "incest" involves completed intercourse between people of the opposite sex, who are close blood relatives. The people involved can be of any age, so legal incest could involve an adult brother and sister for example. In Canada, less than a dozen cases are prosecuted under the formal incest statute each year.

"Incestuous abuse" is, however, much more common, and involves sexual assault upon a male or female child or adolescent by someone who occupies a family role in relation to that individual. That role could be of stepfather, and the blood relationship itself is not crucial. These types of abuse tend to be the most serious and the most damaging, since the child is often trapped by the family member and coerced into a long-term relationship which becomes increasingly intrusive the longer it continues. The consequences for behaviour and mental health of the victim can be very profound, and there is no doubt that those in child care facilities of various kinds are particularly likely to have such a history. It is crucially important that authorities and alternative caretakers at various levels do not "blame the victim," reinforcing the young person's subjective feeling of badness.

Meiselman offers wise insights into the sufferings of the victims of incestuous abuse, and her book contains numerous case histories of both adult victims, and of children in therapy. Three chapters in this book will be of special value for child and youth care workers: that on assessing children's reports on sexual assault by a family member; the chapter on treating child and adolescent victims; and that on treating male survivors. The term "survivor" implies that the former victim can overcome the experience of trauma, regain self-esteem and indeed can start to self-actualize, making the most of their potential.

The sections on group therapy for adolescent victims/survivors are particularly useful. And the final chapter on avoiding therapist burnout could be invaluable to some child and youth care workers!

REFERENCES

Bagley, C., & King, K. (1990). *Child Sexual Abuse: The Search for Healing.* New York: Routledge.

Mary Wells. *Canada's Law on Sexual Abuse.* Ottawa: Department of Justice, Government of Canada, 1990, 117 pp.

Although many of the Badgley Committee's important recommendations were not acted upon (see R. Dawson, "Child sexual abuse, juvenile prostitution and child pornography: The federal response," *Journal of Child and Youth Care, 1987, 3*(2), 19–52), a number of important legal changes have been implemented, both as a result of Badgley's recommendations and as a result of the new Canadian Charter of Rights, which requires that legal processing and penalties shall be similar for the sexes.

This book by Mary Wells is an extraordinarily helpful guide to these legal changes. After a useful historical introduction the author outlines the 16 sexual offenses in the Criminal Code of Canada that can apply to child sexual abuse. Besides these offences there are other elements or general principles in law: regardless of what happens, or the age of the parties, sexual activity *without consent* is always a crime. Children under 12 are never considered able to consent to sexual activity, and the whole thrust of law is to reinforce the fact that children need to be protected in various ways.

Children of 12 or more but under 14 are deemed unable to consent to sexual acts except under specific circumstances involving voluntary activity with close in age peers. Those who are 14 or more but under 18 are protected from sexual exploitation, and their consent is *not* valid if the person touching them for a sexual purpose is in a position of trust or authority, or they are in a relationship of dependency with that person. For example, a 17-year-old would be unable to give consent in law to a sexual relationship with, say, a 22-year-old child care worker in a facility where he or she was resident.

It is not a defence in charges of sexual assault for the accused to say that he or she believed the young person was older than 18. The person accused of the crime has to prove that all "reasonable steps" were taken, such as asking for identification showing proof of age. There are new laws addressing child prostitution. It is now illegal for anyone to exchange sex for money or favours with anyone under 18, and the onus is on the adult who seeks this sexual relationship to establish proof of age.

There are some important new rules regarding child witnesses, making it easier for children's evidence of sexual abuse to be heard in court. Corroboration (supporting evidence) is no longer required for the child's evidence to be accepted. The child (or young adult) can also give evidence about events which took place many months or even years before. The child's reputation (e.g., alleged sexual behaviour with other people than the accused) may not be introduced into court, or be broached in cross-examination.

Courts now have stronger powers to protect the identity of victims, and to exclude the public and press from hearings. The nature of "an oath or solemn affirmation" is clarified. Children simply have to agree to "tell the truth." Child victims can testify from behind a screen, or in another room and be seen by the judge on closed-circuit television, to prevent the anguish of having to face the alleged abuser, and the effect on testimony which such confrontation might have. Videotaped interviews with the victim soon after an assault can also be introduced as evidence. The right of defence counsel to cross-examine the child is not undermined by any of these arrangements.

In the revised Criminal Code, there now exist three summary offences with which an alleged sexual offender against a child can be charged. "Summary offenders" are tried in provincial court before a judge only, and have maximum penalties of a $2,000 fine, six months in jail, or both. The three summary offences are exposing genitals to a child, vagrancy with a child which exposes them to sexual risk, and indecent acts (not involving touching the child). Various kinds of sexual exploitation, sexual touching, sexual intercourse, incest, organizing a child's prostitution, and aggravated sexual assault are treated as indictable offences, with the potential for much more serious penalties. An alleged offender who is more than 12 but less than 18 will be dealt with in Family Court under provisions of the Young Offenders Act, and is liable to much less stringent penalties. Judges in youth or family court in various jurisdictions have considerable powers to order treatment for the young sexual offender.

This book spells out in detail new Criminal Code offences, such as Section 151 on sexual interference; Section 152 on invitation to sexual touching; Section 153 on sexual exploitation of a young person; Section 159 on anal intercourse; Section 170 on parent or guardian procuring sexual activity in a child.

What is crucially important, of course, is how prosecutors and judges interpret these new laws, and rules of evidence. In some parts of Canada (e.g., parts of Ontario) it can take more than a year for a case of child sexual assault to come to trial, and eventually the case may be dismissed because the long waiting time has violated the rights of the accused! During this long waiting period nobody may attend to the needs of the victim. A demonstration project funded by federal health and welfare and organized by the London Family Clinic has shown that rehearsal in court procedures (though not rehearsal of evidence, which is legally inappropriate), and psychological support for the child witness reduces stress in the witness, and reduces drop-out by the witness before the date of trial. This demonstration project deserves replication across Canada.

❧ ❧ ❧

William Friedrich. *Psychotherapy of Sexually Abused Children and Their Families.* New York: W.W. Norton and Company, 1990, 318 pp.

The author of this book is a psychologist, and a consultant at the

Mayo Clinic in Rochester, Minnesota, where he has had extensive experience in treating sexually abused children.

The great merit of this book is its comprehensiveness. It covers all aspects of assessment and treatment of sexually abused children and their families. Among the topics addressed are an understanding of the impact of sexual trauma on children; how such trauma interacts with other developmental problems, and has different sequels according to the child's age and developmental status; methods of comprehensive case management for the victim and his or her family; individual treatment with the child; understanding and treating the family; group therapy with child and adolescent victims; hypnotherapy with sexually abused children; management of sexually reactive and aggressive behaviours; and the role of the therapist in coming to terms with his or her own feelings and experience of sexuality and family conflict.

One of the dilemmas for the child care worker in the residential care setting is that a sexually abused child may act out sexually, both with other children and with the worker. The worker has to act with great caution when this happens, immediately giving a report of any seductive or assaultive behaviour to colleagues and supervisors. The child has to learn that touching, relating and caring can be done in safety and without sexual content.

Given the prevalence of child sexual abuse (some 8% of females and 5% of males in the general population will have experienced prolonged, or serious sexual abuse in childhood) and the known link of the experience of such abuse to a sexual interest in children as an adult, it is probable that some child care workers will themselves still be struggling with their own experience of victimization. It is important that they come to terms with that victimization before working with children. The combination of a child care worker who faces the abyss of pedophilia and a previously victimized child who can only express affection in sexualized ways could well be a disastrous one.

Child care workers need comprehensive training and support in working with sexually abused children. This book is an essential acquisition for child care educators and for all child care institutions since it can be of significant help in a variety of educational programs.

❧ ❧ ❧

Lawrence S. Wissaw. *Child Advocacy for the Clinician: An Approach to Child Abuse and Neglect.* Baltimore: Williams and Wilkins, 1990. 242 pp.

This book is addressed to physicians, and addresses all aspects of child abuse and neglect. For the non-medical worker, it is a useful source of reference, indicating the kinds of concerns which physicians may have and the expertise they can offer child welfare and child care workers. The chapter on "Children as Abusers" is especially interesting for the child and youth care profession. Wissaw makes the point that much abusive sexual behaviour by children and youth is dismissed as part of a normal developmental phase: but this is a mistaken assumption. Although children often engage in mutual sexual display and exploration with close-in-age peers and siblings, this behaviour is clearly distinguished from some types of sexual abuse and assault which children and youth may engage in. In dealing with these young abusers, proceed with compassion and care, Wissaw advises, for many of these perpetrators have been victims themselves. Condemning the young abuser (as opposed to treating him) may close off forever an important therapeutic window to his own experience of victimization.

❧ ❧ ❧

George Barnard, A. Kenneth Fuyller, Lynn Robbins and Theodore Shaw. *The Child Molester: An Integrated Approach to Evaluation and Treatment.* New York: Brunner/Mazel, 1990. 264 pp.

This book represents a valuable addition to the sparse but growing literature on those who sexually abuse children. The book is written by a multidisciplinary team, and covers all aspects of the problem from historical perspectives, typology, developmental issues, residential treatment programs, legal and forensic issues, and clinical implications for therapists of various kinds.

The book is useful reading for those concerned with child treatment in residential centres. The research makes it clear that the roots of child molesting by adults have their roots in childhood developmental problems. For most adults who become persistent child abusers, their potentially deviant interests and fantasies have surfaced by age 12 or 13. This is a crucial time to begin treatment of any child or adolescent offender.

Research cited in this book indicates that child and adolescent sexual assaults tend to be less efficient (and less likely to result in penetration of the victim); and less organized than the assaults made by adults. This does *not* mean that such assaults should be taken less seriously. Often (in up to 50% of cases) adult offenders (who are male in about 95% of cases) were themselves victims of child sexual abuse. The victim to abuser cycle is an important one which child and youth care therapists must address.

❧ ❧ ❧

Rix Rogers. *Reaching for Solutions: Report of the Special Advisor to the Minister of National Health and Welfare on Child Sexual Abuse in Canada.* Ottawa: The Queen's Printer, 1990. 190 pp.

A government commission on child sexual abuse in Canada (chaired by Dr. Robin Badgley of the University of Toronto) published its report in

1984, and set in motion a number of important policy and legal changes. Included among those changes was the appointment of a special advisor to the Minister. This advisor, Rix Rogers, spent several years visiting various agencies and service providers in Canada, and, as a result, has produced this lucidly written and hard-hitting report which will, hopefully, influence Canadian policy in the years to come.

The Report offers 74 recommendations, including one that the federal government issue a statement of what action it intends to take in response to the Report's recommendations, within six months. Some government organizations have set up special family violence committees; and a special interdepartmental committee has been set up to consider the 74 recommendations of the Rogers Report.

Among other important recommendations are the following:

- A National Resource Centre on Child Abuse be established by the federal government.
- Five to seven regional Centres for the Prevention of Child Abuse should be set up across Canada.
- Key areas for government action are public awareness and primary prevention; justice issues; healing and treatment; and aboriginal concerns.
- Protocol be developed in each local community to facilitate inter-disciplinary cooperation in serving the needs of sexually abused children.
- Churches (including their youth organizations) develop policies and procedures for responding appropriately to the problem of child sexual abuse.
- Crown attorneys should prosecute in every case of known child sexual abuse when the evidence merits, provided that the prosecution would not unduly traumatize the child.
- All police officers and their supervisors receive training in issues related to child sexual abuse and family violence. Relevant training should be at least a week long.
- Sentencing judges should receive information about the damaging long-term effects of child sexual abuse.
- Addressing the needs of adult survivors of child sexual abuse should be an important objective for provinces and territories; self-help and other community-based groups should be eligible for cost-sharing with the federal government.
- Provincial and territorial governments develop methods of providing psychiatric consultation services in community-based settings. ("Psychiatric" is interpreted in the widest sense, including a range of mental health workers, including child and youth care personnel.)

- Professional schools and colleges should ensure that those who will work with children are competent to respond to cases of child sexual abuse disclosure; and humane child-centred approach practice methods should be developed.
- Governments at all levels should set up task forces and committees to examine the issue of child sexual abuse of children in institutional settings, of very young children, disabled and disturbed children, and new Canadians.

This review is written seven months after the Rogers Report was published and no public statement by government (apart from that implicit in releasing the Report) has been made. Recommendation 73 of that report was that the federal government should announce within six months what action they intended to take on the recommendations. Coincidentally, since I began writing this review, federal Health and Welfare have issued a press statement saying that a special group has been set up "to promote discussion and to explore ways of implementing Mr. Rogers' recommendations directed at the non-governmental sector." Within the federal government itself, the Department of Health and Welfare has assumed responsibility for coordinating responses between departments. A few weeks after this statement the Federal Government issued a number of important response papers, which are reviewed below.

❧ ❧ ❧

Health and Welfare Canada. *Family Violence Initiative*. Ottawa: Government of Canada, 1991, 4 pp.
Health and Welfare Canada. *Family Violence - Background Paper*. Ottawa: Government of Canada, 1991, 20 pp.
Health and Welfare Canada. *Family Violence - Situation Paper*. Ottawa: Government of Canada, 1991, 12 pp.
Health and Welfare Canada. *Federal Response to 'Reaching for Solutions: Report of the Special Advisor on Child Sexual Abuse*, Ottawa: Government of Canada, 1991, 16 pp.

These four booklets, issued in February 1991 as part of a single package, represent an important initiative in the Canadian government's response to the policy initiatives and changes set in motion by the report of the Committee on Sexual Offences Against and Youth (the Badgley Committee) which addressed its report to the federal government in 1984. Not only do they contain government's response to the Rogers Report recommendations (reviewed above) which address the domain of competence of the federal government, but they also lay the foundation for important new funding initiatives for family violence prevention and treatment.

Basically, the government's response to the recommendations of the Rogers Report are favourable and the large majority of recommendations are accepted in principle for some kind of action (though not necessarily to the full extent that Rogers advocated). A number of recommendations will not be acted on, however, mainly because they are seen to be the exclusive jurisdiction of provincial child welfare authorities and solicitors general. Clearly the federal government of Canada is in a considerable dilemma in initiating radical new programs at a time when the provinces are increasingly assertive about their exclusive rights in political and social domains.

Nevertheless, the federal government has committed $136 million of "new" money to initiatives for the prevention and treatment of child abuse and family violence, particularly in the health and social service fields. The money, to be spent over four years, is directed to six areas of action: mobilizing communities to prevent child and family violence; helping professionals and front-line workers through manuals and training programs, with special resources for 2,000 health care and social service workers in Native Indian and Inuit communities; improving treatment and support for victims, through initiatives cost-shared with the provinces and territories; creating a shared information system of research and best-practice across the country; providing a better national information base about the extent and nature of family violence in Canada, through special research surveys; and the better coordination of the work of criminal justice, health and social service systems in meeting the needs of victims of family violence and child abuse.

It is clear from these government statements of future policy that child abuse and family violence is a priority issue in terms of budget allocation in a time of cutbacks in many other areas of spending. The ambitious program of spending announced some five years ago on preschool child care, for example, has now been formally abandoned. The government, not surprisingly, now wishes to husband its scarce social service dollars in the areas where suffering is greatest.

❧ ❧ ❧

Thom McGuire and Faye Grant. *Understanding Child Sexual Abuse.* Toronto: Butterworths, 1991. 48 pp.

This short book, marketed at about nine dollars, is intended for wide distribution amongst "professionals working with children." The problem is that the book tries to do too much, attempting to cover the whole field of child sexual abuse, its nature, effects, the treatment and care of victims, processing of offenders, coordination of professional responses, and more. This cannot possibly be done with any adequacy in 48 pages, and the danger is that the front-line worker who reads this book may think that he or she has acquired an adequate knowledge in this field. There is nothing on residential care and treatment.

The book itself is well written, and could easily have been three times its existing length. At that length, this might well have been a useful book for practitioners. In its present form the book would be of more use in high school libraries, rather than in the hands of front-line professionals.

❧ ❧ ❧

Margaret A. Michaud. *Dead End: Homeless Teenagers — A Multi-Service Approach.* Calgary: Detselig Enterprises, 1988. 138 pp.

Street kids are often refugees from abuse in the home — emotional, physical and sexual. On the streets they are at risk for further abuse, and the predations of pimps and pushers. Many, both male and female, become recruited into juvenile prostitution where they are subjected to further, yet more horrendous abuses by clients, pimps and authorities of various kinds. Mental and physical health of these young people, many of whom have been resident in conventional child care institutions, is often profoundly at risk.

Margaret Michaud outlines five rather successful responses to street kids. The first program, Avenue 15, arose from a research initiative first described in this journal (K. Kufeldt and M. Nimmo, "Kids on the street — they have something to say: A survey of runaway and homeless youth," *Journal of Child and Youth Care*, 1987, *3* (2), 63–70). Kufeldt and her team, working in cooperation with the Boys and Girls Clubs of Calgary, surveyed 408 young people who inhabited the downtown core of Calgary for permanent or temporary periods during a six-month period. A major finding was the existence of a sub-group (122 of the 408) described as "ins and outer" — adolescents who left home for a temporary period (often several times) but who had returned home before, or planned to return. This is a crucial group with which to work and try and resolve family and other problems, and for this purpose, Avenue 15 offers temporary accommodation, counselling and help to a number of teenagers who are at the stage where they have just begun to run from home.

The next program described is the Toronto Street Outreach Services (S.O.S.), a program with three aspects: four full-time street workers talking particularly to young prostitutes, and connecting them with various kinds of support and counselling; an office drop-in centre with a youth worker; and a high support phase, with a personal youth worker attached to an individual for up to 15 hours a week. The young person has access to a peer support group and co-op boarding house. About half of all clients have had some prior involvement with the child welfare system, and many have been in residential child care facilities at some phase of their lives. Descriptive statistics on 835 clients illustrate both the desperate need for a service like this, and its potential success.

The Downtown Eastside Youth Activities Society (DEYAS) described by Michaud is based in Vancouver, and focuses on a low-income area with a high proportion of Native adolescents who are at risk of being drawn into various illegal activities. Unemployment and father-absent families are frequent facts of life. Youth workers with DEYAS identify youth on the street who appear to be at risk, and offer a variety of help and support services including the possibility of return to Reserve or rural community.

Orion Street Youth Theatre Project in Seattle is supported by private industrial sponsors, and offers educational and recreational programs for youth aged 16 to 21 who are at risk in various ways. One problem of prior abuse is that it leads to school dropout and impairs the occupational skills and life chances of the young person. Individual counselling is available for the youth throughout the project, as well as group work. Theatre training and drama productions seem to be both recreational and therapeutic.

The Bridge is a Boston-based program founded in 1970, and serves runaway and homeless clients aged 14 to 21. A special focus is the growing number of pregnant teenagers and young mothers, with counselling and education which focuses on giving this group adequate support for good child care.

As Michaud makes clear, these are by no means the only programs available in North America — each is representative of a different kind of model, but all appear to be effective in at least some of their goals. A chronic problem is that of adequate funding for continuous programming. The irony is that these important preventive programs can save various public systems (health, social services, criminal justice) many thousands of dollars for a few dollars spent in prevention, support and education.

W.L. Marshall and Sylvia Barrett. *Criminal Conduct: Why Sex Offenders Go Free.* Toronto: Doubleday Canada Limited, 1990. 220 pp.

Bill Marshall is director of the Sexual Behaviour Clinic at Kingston, Ontario, and Sylvia Barrett is a freelance writer. Together they have put together a comprehensive and very readable account of the numerous problems in engaging and treating those who commit sexual offences against adults and children.

First of all, the authors are quite honest about the failures of treatment as well as the general lack of treatment programs. In the face of such problems, judges and parole boards are often forced to let offenders "go free" without treatment. But of course, many of these treated or treated by inadequate programs, may well reoffend. Adolescence is a particularly crucial time for intensive treatment of sexual offenders (and indeed of victims who might go on to become offenders).

But treatment programs in Canada and in many parts of the United States for adolescents are conspicuous by their absence.

The case for treatment of sexual offenders, despite a lack of basic knowledge of why some men offend, is powerful. Consider the following quotation from Marshall and Barrett's book in which they describe the cost-effectiveness of the Kingston Clinic:

> The reoffence rate among men who molested other people's daughters was 25 percent lower than in the untreated group, indicating that of every one hundred men treated at the Kingston Clinic, twenty-five would have committed other sex crimes if they had been left untreated. Since the untreated child molesters who did reoffend averaged two offenders each, we can assume that about fifty children were saved from becoming victims. Furthermore, since it costs the government about $200,000 for each convicted repeat offender, we can extrapolate that it would save 25 times that amount, or more than $4 million, over the two years it takes the clinic to treat one hundred offenders. (During a two-year period, the program itself receives only $120,000 in provincial government grants.) (p. 161)

The rest of the book is written in a clear style (like the above quotation), and although this is essentially a non-academic book, intended to be read by the general public, it does actually cover all the fundamentals of research in this area in a way which satisfies the expert (which this reviewer purports to be). This book can be warmly recommended to professionals at a variety of levels, and to the general reader interested in this important social issue. The numerous case histories make this a particularly interesting book.

Chris Bagley
The University of Calgary

Journal of Child and Youth Care Special Issue Pages 153 – 156
 ISSN 0840-982X

Other Reviews

Catherine Garvey. *Play*. Cambridge, Massachusetts: Harvard University Press, 1990, 141 pp.

This is the second, enlarged edition of *Play*, which was first published in 1977. This book is part of the Developing Child series of books that focuses on research on child development and its implications for policy formulation.

Play presents the findings of Garvey's observational study of preschool children, which focused on how, in the absence of adults, children interact, communicate, and play with each other. Garvey also incorporates the findings of many other recent studies of children's play. She argues convincingly that play has important consequence for the social, emotional, and cognitive development of children.

In Chapter 1 the author reviews various theories of the meaning and function of children's play. She presents an understanding of play as behaviour in the simulative mode, wherein there is a non-literal orientation to experience that allows for behaviours to be practiced while buffering the child from the normal consequences of imperfect achievement. Garvey reviews briefly the results of her own research and argues convincingly that the thought and social life of the pre-school child may not be as egocentric as previous theory and research has suggested. She suggests that play is primarily social in nature and that solitary play is secondary.

Following a brief consideration of the parallels between play and the emergence of smiling and laughter in infancy in Chapter 2, specific forms of play behaviour that emerge as the child matures are examined in Chapters 3 through 7. These chapters focus on play with various resources or materials: (a) motion and interaction; (b) objects; (c) language; (d) social materials (e.g., roles, situations, etc.); and (e) rules. Chapter 8 examines the phenomenon of ritualized play, which can be based on any resource or material. Throughout these chapters Garvey explains and gives examples of how, as the child's world and abilities expand, the different types of play emerge, develop, and integrate into more complex forms of play.

Chapters 9 and 10 are new to the second edition of this book. Chapter 9 focuses on social influences, particularly that of the family, on children's play. In addition, the complex phenomenon of social pretend play is explored in this chapter. Chapter 10 examines gender differences in play (which do not seem to be changing as yet in spite of social changes brought about by the women's movement) and the relationship between play and both social and literacy skills.

Play is a well-written book that clearly documents the systematic, rule-governed nature of play and its significance for children's development and general well-being. Given that an increasing number of young children are enrolled in daycare programs and that parents' anxieties about their children's development may thus be heightened, it seems particularly timely to stress the importance of letting children be children. The one disappointment in this book is the paucity of practical suggestions to enable parents, educators, and child care professionals to encourage and facilitate children's play. Nevertheless, this is a valuable book for anyone concerned with the developing child.

Tiffany Field. *Infancy*. Cambridge, Massachusetts: Harvard University Press, 1990, 170 pp.

Infancy is one of approximately twenty books in The Developing Child series, which is edited by Jerome Bruner and Michael Cole. The intent of each book in this series is to disseminate the results of recent research on child development to child care professionals and parents.

This book provides a very useful summary and synthesis of recent research on child development in the first two years of life. The primary focus of the book is on the social-emotional development of infants, although perceptual, motor, and cognitive development are also discussed. More specific topics that are addressed include high-risk infants and the effects of infant daycare. Two major themes emerge in this book: (a) that infants possess far more sophisticated skills than generally recognized, and (b) that many infants are amazingly resilient and invulnerable to stress.

Chapter One provides an orientation to infancy as a field of study. Field argues convincingly for the need to supplement traditional experimental laboratory studies of infants with naturalistic observations that are more ecologically meaningful. She details some of the unique problems involved in studying infants and she explains how multiple measures of infant response (e.g., visual behaviour, heart rate, parents' reports) can help to overcome some of these problems.

In Chapter Two, Field discusses fetal development, the birth process, and the newborn. The author explains how studies have established that infants develop perceptual skills such as hearing, feeling, and tasting in utero. She then discusses how the newborn's well-developed abilities, including the surprising ability to imitate facial expressions, are helpful in the social interactions that begin at birth.

Chapter Three provides a discussion of the infant's motor development, learning processes, and memory. Field reviews how the sequence of motor milestones is relatively invariant and how only slight variations in the timing of the onset of motor skills can be affected by environmental input. She explains how motor skill development is critical for perceptual and cognitive development and how all of these developmental areas are intertwined with social-emotional development.

The central topic of social-emotional development is covered in Chapter Four. Field discusses how infants' abilities to make facial expressions and to discriminate faces and voices, and parents' abilities to engage in "infantized" behaviour, are mutually reinforcing. She addresses the important fact that there are individual differences among infants with regard to emotional responsivity and temperament. Field cites evidence to suggest that such differences derive from genetic background and prenatal/perinatal experiences and that they tend to persist into adulthood. Attachment and the associated phenomena of stranger fear and separation stress are also discussed in this chapter. Field differentiates the caregiving provided by mothers of securely-attached infants from that provided by mothers of insecurely-attached infants, however she is careful to acknowledge that infants' characteristics can also contribute to attachment difficulties. Field also provides an interesting critique of the "strange situation" procedure through which attachment is usually studied. She argues convincingly that attachment might be better studied in non-stressful situations.

Chapter Five addresses the controversial issue of infant daycare. Field critiques studies that suggest that infants experiencing daycare in the first year are adversely affected in the areas of attachment and preschool social adjustment. She notes that such studies are based on data from low-quality daycare centres and questionable measures of attachment. Furthermore, Field cites other studies that show infant daycare results in an enhancement of social skills and does not negatively affect attachment behaviour. She stresses that continuity and quality of care are the crucial factors. Field also presents findings from studies of infant-peer interactions that suggest that infants are sociable with their peers from an early age and that they develop attachments to peers.

In Chapter Six, Field reviews the literature on infants that are at risk for developmental problems due to prenatal (e.g., maternal disease, anxiety, drug/alcohol abuse), birth, (e.g., premature/postmature delivery, low birth weight, congenital abnormalities), and postnatal (e.g., maternal postpartum depression, neglect/abuse) factors. She provides an insightful explanation of the vicious cycle of problematic interactions that can easily occur between mothers and their high-risk infants. Most importantly, Field also discusses how "interactive coaching" can be used as an intervention to modify such disturbed interactional sequences.

Field concludes the book with a brief "Afterword" in which she emphasizes the resiliency and coping abilities of infants. She discusses how a positive social orientation, autonomy, and risk-taking seem to be protective factors that are characteristic of infants that cope well with stress. Field also suggests that parents who tend to be overprotective might better foster their children's coping abilities by allowing them to engage in more risk-taking behaviour and by challenging them to use their own resources.

Infancy is a well-written, informative book that provides the reader with a wealth of up-to-date references on early child development research as well as some very practical suggestions for facilitating children's social-emotional development. As such, it should be of interest to childcare professionals, students, and parents alike.

Nicholas Coady
The University of Calgary

The JOURNAL OF CHILD AND YOUTH CARE is primarily intended for the professional child care worker. It is recognized, however, that the issues of child caring are universal, and the JOURNAL is committed to the dissemination of information and knowledge for the benefit of all individuals who assume responsibility for the well-being of children. Articles covering a broad range of perspectives will be considered for publication, but special attention will be given to manuscripts submitted by front-line practitioners. Authors should refer to the Information for Authors page for submission requirements.

Subscriptions

The regular institutional rate is $71.50 per year. The professional rate for members of child care associations is $38.50. The rate for non-affiliated subscribers is $49.50. Canadian subscribers must add 7% GST. Cheques should be made payable to the University of Calgary Press. Payments should be in Canadian or U.S. funds.

Back Issues

Information regarding the availability and prices of back issues may be obtained from the Calgary office of the JOURNAL.

Change of Address

Six weeks' advance notice must be given in notifying a change of address.

Advertising

Current rates and specifications may be obtained from the Calgary office of the JOURNAL.

Reviews

Publications and other materials submitted for review should be addressed to the editors at the JOURNAL office.

Information For Authors

The Journal of Child and Youth Care welcomes the submission of manuscripts on all subjects related to the field of child care. Although a broad range of material will be considered for publication, preference will be given to applications, training strategies, and program designs. Special attention will be given to submissions relating directly to child care practice, including case study analyses. As the Journal is primarily for the benefit of practitioners, authors should avoid unnecessary jargon and excessive use of statistics.

Manuscripts

Manuscripts should be submitted in triplicate to the Editors, Journal of Child and Youth Care, 2266 Woodpark Avenue S.W., Calgary, Alberta, T2W 2Z8. Articles should be double spaced on $8^1/2$" by 11" paper and not exceed 20 pages in length. An abstract (on a separate sheet) of approximately 100 words should accompany each submission. Since any articles may be reviewed anonymously by the Consulting Editors, the title **only** should appear on the front page. Authorship, including brief biographical information, should be attached on a separate sheet. When a manuscript has been accepted for publication, each author will be asked to submit a head-and-shoulders photograph of reproducible quality. None of the submitted materials will be returned unless specifically requested.

Style

Style of presentation should conform to the guidelines outlined in the *Publication Manual of the American Psychological Association* (Third Edition, 1984). Although no submission will be rejected purely for stylistic reasons, the editors reserve the right to return any manuscript for additional work. Authors requiring editorial assistance in this regard should indicate their request in a covering letter.

Originality

Originality of material is the responsibility of the primary author. Previously published material may only be submitted and published in the Journal with the expressed consent of the Editors.